144 THOUSAND

and Speaking

IN TONGUES

MELVIN WINFREY

144 THOUSAND AND SPEAKING IN TONGUES
Copyright © 2024 by Melvin Winfrey

ISBN: 979-8992128017 (hc)
ISBN: 979-8992128000 (sc)
ISBN: 979-8992128024 (e)

Library of Congress Control Number: 2024925701

Melvin Winfrey

melwinfrey2009@gmail.com

Revelation 14:1

"And I looked, and lo, a Lamb stood on the mount Zion, and with him a hundred forty and four thousand, having his Father's name written in their foreheads." Now the hundred and forty four thousand is all the saints that shall be saved, from the beginning until the end.

Now it divides where it says:

"A Lamb stood on the mount Zion," for more information turn to Revelation 5:5, "And one of the elders saith unto me, weep not: behold, the Lion of the tribe of Juda, the Root of David, hath prevailed to open the book, and to loose the seven seals thereof." Jesus Christ stood with the hundred forty and four thousand. The hundred forty and four thousand is all the people that had died, from thousands of years ago. Until Jesus Christ come, and the one's that remain alive, when He come.

They are all the saints from the beginning of time until Christ come back. They are the first-fruits. They are the hundred forty and four thousand.

Now the next dividing in Revelation 14:1, where it says:

"A hundred forty and four thousand," let's go to Revelation 7:4, "And I heard the number of them which were sealed: and there were sealed a hundred and forty and four thousand of all the tribes of the children of Israel."

Now you see in this verse 4 John heard the number of them, which were sealed. He did not see the people that were sealed. And they came from all the tribes of the children of Israel, and the Gentiles are graffed into the tribes of the children of Israel, the one's that are saved, and they are one in the body of Christ.

1

Now read Romans 11:17 on down. I will read a couple of verses. Verse 19:

"Thou wilt say then, the branches were broken off, that I might be graffed in."

Now you see, the Gentiles are grafted into the tribes. Now verse 20:

"Well; because of unbelief they were broken off, and thou standest by faith. Be not high-minded, but fear:" The Gentiles were grafted in because of Israel of unbelief so the Gentiles were graffed into the tribes.

Now this is what you read about in Revelation 7:9

"After this I beheld, and lo, a great multitude, which no man could number, of all nations, and kindreds, and people, and tongues, stood before the throne, and before the Lamb, clothed with white robes, and palms in their hands:"

Now after John heard the numbers, which were sealed, and then after that John beheld. Now that mean he looked at the people, gaze upon the people and it was a great multitude from all nations. So that mean Israel included and this is the same group of people of those twelve tribes of the children of Israel, the hundred and forty and four thousand. You see, first John heard the number, which were sealed in verse 4. But in verse 9, John looks at the people that were before the throne. It was a great multitude which no man could number because a hundred and forty and four thousand people is a great multitude of people. Just by looking at the people, you cannot number how much is there. Only God knows. Just like if you walk into the super dorm then you hear the man on the speaker says, "There is eighty thousand and one hundred twenty one people in here." Now you only heard how many people were in the super dorm, you did not see the people. Now that's the same thing as what John heard. Now after you get where you can see the people, you say, This is a great multitude, which no man could number.

You see in verse 4, John heard the number of them which were sealed: the hundred and forty and four thousand. Now in verse 9, he looks at the people, the same hundred and forty and four thousand, and it was a great multitude from all nations. And that is the same hundred and forty and four thousand people of the children of Israel from the twelve tribes.

I have described what John saw in verse 9. Now I hope you all out there understand what I have explained to you. Because there are only going to be a hundred and forty and four thousand people, of the first-fruit will be saved.

Now back to Revelation 14:1, where it says:

"having his Father's name written in their foreheads."

Let's turn to Revelation 7:3 and Revelation 13:16. Now Revelation 7:3 reads:

"Saying, hurt not the earth, neither the sea, nor the trees, till we have sealed the servants of our God in their foreheads."

Now all the saints will have God the Father name written in their foreheads.

Revelation 13:16

"And he causeth all, both small and great, rich and poor, free and bond, to receive a mark in their right hand, or in their foreheads;" You see Satan will cause his people to receive a mark in their forehead or in their hand that no man might buy or sell, save he that had the mark, or the name of the beast, or the number of his name.

Revelation 14:2

"And I heard a voice from heaven, as the voice of many waters, and as the voice of a great thunder: and I heard the voice of harpers harping with their harps:"

Now the voice of many waters, that is the Lord Jesus Christ. Now it divides where it says:

"As the voice of many waters,"

3

Revelation 1:15.

"And his feet like unto fine brass, as if they burned in a furnace; and his voice as the sound of many waters." Now you see this is the Lord Jesus Christ voice as the sound of many waters. Now the next dividing occurs in verse 2 where it says: "harpers harping with their harps:" For more detail turn to Revelation 5:8

"And when he had taken the book, the four beasts, and four and twenty elders fell down before the Lamb, having everyone of them harps, and golden vials full of odors, which are the prayers of saints."

Now before the throne shall be "the voice of harpers harping with their harps:" Now verse 3:

"And they sung as it were a new song before the throne, and before the four beasts, and the elders: and no man could learn that song but the hundred and forty and four thousand, which were redeemed from the earth."

Now all the saints from the beginning to the end, when Jesus Christ come back.

Now Revelation 14:4

"These are they which were not defiled with women; for they are virgins. These are they which follow the Lamb whithersoever he goeth. These were redeemed from among men, being the first-fruits unto God and to the Lamb."

Now these are the hundred and forty and four thousand that are from all nations, the twelve tribe, all the tribes of the children of Israel. Now it divides to verse 4 where it says "they". It goes to 2 Corinthians 11:2

"For I am jealous over you with godly jealousy: for I have espoused you to one husband, that I may present you as a chaste virgin to Christ."

Now the saints are a virgin to Christ, we are a new creation in Christ. Now the next dividing is in verse 4 where it says:

"Which follow the Lamb whithersoever he goeth." For a better understanding turn to: Revelation 3:4 Revelation 7:15, 17 Revelation 17:14 Now Revelation 3:4

"Thou hast a few names even in Sardis which have not defiled their garments; and they shall walk with me in white: for they are worthy." You see they shall walk with the Lord in white. That means they follow the Lamb whithersoever he goeth.

Now Revelation 7:15, 17

"Therefore are they before the throne of God, and serve him day and night in his temple: and he that sitteth on the throne shall dwell among them." So they shall be with the Lord. Verse 17:

"For the Lamb which is in the midst of the throne shall feed them, and shall lead them unto living fountains of water: and God shall wipe away all tears from their eyes." Jesus Christ will be among his saints.

Now Revelation 17:14

"These shall make war with the Lamb, and the Lamb shall overcome them; for he is Lord of lords, and King of kings; and they that are with him are called, and chosen, and faithful." And the saints that are with him, they follow the Lamb whithersoever he goeth. Now the next dividing is in verse 4 where it says:

"Were redeemed from among men," it goes to Revelation 5:9, and I will show you, by the scripture, the hundred and forty and four thousand. They are from all nations and they "were redeemed from among men".

Now Revelation 5:9

"And they sung a new song, saying, Thou art worthy to take the book, and to open the seals thereof: for thou wast slain, and hast redeemed us to God by thy blood out of every kindred, and tongue, and people, and nation;" Now you see the hundred and forty and four thousand, they are from every people and nations. Now the next dividing is in Revelation 14:4, where it say:

"being the first-fruits unto God and to the Lamb." Now the saints are the first fruits unto God and to the Lamb from the Old Testament, and from the New Testament. They are the first-fruits unto God and to the Lamb. They are the hundred and forty and four thousand that are from all nations. Now "being the first-fruits unto God and to the Lamb" it goes to James 1:18

"Of his own will begat he us with the word of truth, that we should be a kind of first-fruits of his creatures." Now the Lord begat us with the word of truth. The saints are the first-fruits from the new testament and from the old testament. Now I will show you by the scripture in James 1:18 where it says:

"first-fruits of his creatures." It goes to Jeremiah 2:3 and Revelation 14:4. Now you see the new testament saints and the old testament saints are the first-fruits of God. Now Jeremiah 2:3

"Israel was holiness unto the LORD, and the first-fruits of his increase: all that devour him shall offend; evil shall come upon them, saith the LORD." Now you see in the old testament Israel was the Lord,first-fruits of his increase. Now in the new testament the same thing, the saints are the first-fruits of his increase. Now in the new testament the saints are Israel. The saints are from all nations, and that is Israel. And that is the hundred and forty and four thousand from all nations. The saints are Israel from all nations. Now Revelation 14:5

"And in their mouth was found no guile: for they are without fault before the throne of God." Now these were all the saints that were before the throne of God from all nations, the saints from the old testament and the new testament. Now it divides where it says

"in their mouth was found no guile:" For more insight turn to Psalms 32:2 and Zephaniah 3:13. Now Psalms 32:2

"Blessed is the man unto whom the LORD imputeth not iniquity, and in whose spirit there is no guile." There was no deceit in them or lies in them. Now Zephaniah 3:13

"The remnant of Israel shall not do iniquity, nor speak lies; neither shall a deceitful tongue be found in their mouth: for they shall feed and lie down, and none shall make them afraid."

They will speak the truth. Now the next dividing is in verse 5 where it says:

"they are without fault before the throne of God." Let's turn to Ephesians 5:27 and Jude 1:24. Now Ephesians 5:27

"That he might present it to himself a glorious church, not having spot or wrinkle, or any such thing; but that it should be holy and without blemish." Now God's church will be without "spot or wrinkle, or any such thing; but that it should be holy and without blemish." And having no fault, now this is God's church. Now Jude 1:24

"Now unto him that is able to keep you from falling, and to present you faultless before the presence of his glory with exceeding joy," Now the church, the saints shall be faultless before the throne of God. Now Revelation 14:6

"And I saw another angel fly in the midst of heaven, having the everlasting gospel to preach unto them that dwell on the earth, and to every nation, and kindred, and tongue, and people," Now the angel will fly in the midst of heaven, having the everlasting gospel to preach unto them that dwell on the earth. Now I believe that is when the two witnesses will prophesy for three and a half years, and the gospel shall be preach unto all nations like Jesus Christ did, he preach the gospel for three and a half years before he died on the cross, and he prophesied. And that is what will happen to the two witnesses, they shall be killed after three and a half years and the antichrist shall set up the abomination that maketh desolate, and that will be an image that he shall set up. Now it divides in verse 6 where it says:

"fly in the midst of heaven," it goes to Revelation 8:13

"And I beheld, and heard an angel flying through the midst of heaven, saying with a loud voice, wo, wo ,wo, to the inhabiters of the earth, by reason of the other voices of the trumpet of the three angels, which are yet to sound!" Now that Angel there was flying in the midst of heaven telling about more suffering and destruction that is coming on the people on the earth. Now the next dividing is in verse 6 where it says

"having the everlasting gospel to preach unto them that dwell on the earth," it goes to Ephesians 3:9,10,11; Titus 1:2. Now' Ephesians 3:9,10,11 I will read verse nine and ten.

"And to make all men see what is the fellowship of the mystery, which from the beginning of the world hath been hid in God, who created all things by Jesus Christ:" Now Paul was preaching the everlasting gospel, that was hid from the beginning of the world, hid in God. Verse 10

"To the intent that now unto the principalities and powers in heavenly places might be known by the church the manifold wisdom of God." Now the rulers, and government, angels and saints that might be known by the church the bountiful wisdom of God. Now Titus 1:2

"In hope of the eternal life, which God, that cannot lie, promised before the world began;" that the gospel shall be preach to the people that dwell on the earth. Now the next dividing in verse 6 where it says:

"And to every nation, and kindred, and tongue, and people," let's go to Revelation 13:7

"And it was given unto him to make war with the saints, and to overcome them: and power was given him over all kindreds, tongues, and nations." Now the gospel shall be preached unto all kindreds, tongues, and nations.

Now Revelation 14:7

"Saying with a loud voice, fear God, and give glory to him; for the hour of his judgment is come: and worship him that made heaven, and earth, and the sea, and the fountains of waters." Now God want you to fear him and give him glory, and worship him because judgment is coining. Now it divides where it says

"Fear God, and give glory to him;" for more detail turn to Revelation 11:18 and Revelation 15:14. Now Revelation 11:18

"And the nations were angry, and thy wrath is come, and the time of the dead, that they should be judged, and that thou shouldst give reward unto thy servants the prophets, and to the saints, and them that fear thy name, small and great; and shouldst destroy them which destroy the earth." Now God will reward them that fear thy name, small and great that are obedience to his words. Now Revelation 15:4

"Who shall not fear thee, O Lord, and glorify thy name For thou only art holy: for all nations shall come and worship before thee: for thy judgments are made manifest." Now all them that the Lord save, they shall fear the Lord and give glory to thy name. Now the next dividing is in verse 7 where it says:

"And worship him that made heaven, and earth, and the sea, and fountains of waters." For more information turn to Nehemiah 9:6.

You can read the rest of these scriptures on your own. Psalms 33:6 Psalms 124:8 Psalms 146:5,6 Acts 14:15 Acts 17:24 Now I am going to read only Nehemiah 9:6:

"Thou, even thou, art LORD alone; thou hast made heaven, the heaven of heavens, with all their host, the earth, and all things that are therein, the seas, and all that is therein, and thou preservest them all; and the host of heaven worshippeth thee." Now we have to worship the Lord, who created the heavens, and the earth, and the fountains of waters. Now Revelation 14:8

"And there followed another angel, saying, Babylon is fallen, is fallen, that great city, because she made all nations drink of the wine of the wrath of her fornication." The nations are starting to drink of the wine of the wrath of her fornication because the people now in the nations are getting angry because of energy prices and food prices. Now it divides where it says in verse 8:

"Babylon is fallen, is fallen," for better understanding let's go Isaiah 21:9, Jeremiah 51:8, Revelation 18:2. Now Isaiah 21:9

9

"And behold, here cometh a chariot of men with a couple of horsemen. And he answered and said, Babylon is fallen, is fallen; and all the graven images of her gods he hath broken unto the ground." Babylon shall fall, and all the graven images. Her statue, like the ones they have in the Catholic Church, an image of Mary. Now this is abomination before God. In Babylon, the prophets prophesy falsely and teach false doctrine, and the priests to teach false doctrine of men. Now Jeremiah 51:8

"Babylon is suddenly fallen and destroyed: howl for her; take balm for her pain, if so be she may be healed." Now this is the first Babylon the one in the Old Testament. It fell suddenly and was destroyed. Now Revelation 18:2

"And he cried mightily with a strong voice, saying, Babylon the great is fallen, is fallen, and is become the habitation of devils, and the hold of every foul spirit, and a cage of every unclean and hateful bird." Now Babylon is fallen, is fallen, and this is Babylon in the New Testament. It "become the habitation of devils, and the hold of every foul spirit, and a cage of every unclean and hateful bird." Now some of these prophets, priests, and teachers say that what America become right now, is a cage of every unclean and hateful bird. The Bible is talking about after Babylon is fallen, is fallen, and is become the habitation of devils, and the hold of every foul spirit, and a cage of every unclean and hateful bird. Now that is after Babylon is fallen, not before. But after it is fallen, it becomes the habitation of devils. Now this false prophet from South Carolina says that the United States is Babylon, but it is not true. He says the U.S. has become an unclean and hateful bird and habitation of the devils now, but that is not true. These things will happen after Babylon is fallen and not before. Now the next dividing is in verse 8 where it says:

"That great city, because she made all nations drink of the wine of the wrath of her fornication." I will read a few verses and the rest, you can read on your own. For better understanding let us turn to Jeremiah 51:7 Revelation 11:8 Revelation 16:19 Revelation 17:2,5 Revelation 18:3,10,18,21 Revelation 19:2 Now Jeremiah 51:7

"Babylon hath been a golden cup in the Lord's hand, that made all the earth drunken: the nations have drunken of her wine; therefore the nations are mad." Now all nations by the Vatican, the Catholic Church, are drunken of her wine of her fornication. The nations are drunk and mad. Now there are two types of people you cannot tell them nothing, a drunken person and a mad person. They will not listen to you, and this is why you cannot tell people anything nowadays. They do not want to listen to you, even though they know you are right. Now Revelation 11:8

"And their dead bodies shall lie in the street of the great city, which spiritually is called Sodom and Egypt, where also our Lord was crucified." The great city is Jerusalem. The Vatican will move their tabernacles around Jerusalem, which spiritually will be called Sodom and Egypt. Now Revelation 16:19

"And the great city was divided into three parts, and the cities of the nations fell: And great Babylon came in remembrance before God, to give unto her the cup of the wine of the fierceness of his wrath." That "great city was divided into three parts, and the cities of the nations fell:" and that will be a great earthquake, and so mighty since men were upon the earth. Now I will read one more dividing Revelation 17:2,5. Verse 2:

"With whom the kings of the earth have committed fornication, and the inhabitants of the earth have been made drunk with the wine of her fornication." The kings of the earth have committed fornication, with the false prophet, the little horn. Now the false prophet will be the pope of Rome. Now the kings of the earth go visit the false prophet at the Vatican, or the false prophet will come to their countries, and the kings of the earth, go visit the false prophet. "And the inhabitants of the earth have been made drunk with the wine of her fornication." Now that church, the Roman Catholic Church, has made the people of the earth drunk. The whole world, all the churches are being unfaithful to God because the kings of the earth, and the people of the earth have committed spiritual fornication with the Roman Catholic Church. And now they are made drunk, and they are mad. Now Revelation 17:5

"And upon her forehead was a name written, MYSTERY, BABYLON THE GREAT, THE MOTHER OF HARLOTS AND ABOMINATIONS OF THE EARTH." So Mystery, Babylon the great, is the mother of Harlots. In order to be a mother, you have to have daughters that mean the rest of these denominational churches. They are under control of the Roman Catholic Church because they teach false doctrine like the Roman Catholic Church. Now back to Revelation 14:9

"And the third angel followed them, saying with a loud voice, If any man worship the beast and his image, and receive his mark in his forehead, or in his hand." Now, if you worship the beast and his image, and receive his mark in your forehead, or in your hand, then you are lost. The wrath of God will come upon you, and you shall be burn with fire forever and ever.

Now rightly dividing the word of truth where it says:

"If any man worship the beast and his image, and receive his mark in his forehead or in his hand," for more detail turn to Revelation 13:14.15,16. Now verse 14

"And deceiveth them that dwell on the earth by the means of those miracles which he had power to do in the sight of the beast; saying to them that dwell on the earth, that they should make an image to the beast, which had the wound by a sword, and did live." Now that second beast, that had two horns like a lamb, was a false prophet. He will tell the people that they should make an image to the beast, which had the wound by a sword, to the beast, which had gotten wounded and did live.

Now verse 15:

"And he had power to give life unto the image of the beast, that the image of the beast should both speak, and cause that as many as would not worship the image of the beast should be killed." That antichrist, that false prophet, will want everybody, all people, kindreds, and tongues, and nations to worship the image of the beast or should be killed. The same thing as NEBUCHADNEZZAR did in Daniel 3:1-6. He causes all nations and people to worship that image that he had set up. Now at the end time it will be the same thing.

Now verse 16

"And he causeth all, both small and great, rich and poor, free and bond, to receive a mark in their right hand, or in their foreheads;" Now that false prophet causeth them which received the mark of the beast, thee antichrist is the false prophet. That false prophet from South Carolina says thee antichrist will not be a religious leader, but a political leader. But that is not true, thee antichrist will be a religious leader and a political leader because that false prophet will tell these ten kings what to do, and the kings of the earth have committed fornication with her, The false prophet gives power unto the ten kings. The false prophet is the head of the Roman Catholic Church, and that will be the last pope that will "come in peaceably, and obtain the kingdom by flatteries." He causeth all to receive a mark in their right hand or in their foreheads; Now everybody won't receive the same thing, some the mark and some the number of his name. But anybody that receives the mark of the beast, they are lost, it is over, and they are lost forever. They will burn forever, the one that received the mark of the beast, in order to buy or sell.

Now Revelation 14:10

"The same shall drink of the wine of the wrath of God, which is poured out without mixture into the cup of his indignation; and he shall be tormented with fire and brimstone in the presence of the holy angels, and in the presence of the Lamb:" The wrath of God shall be upon the people that received the mark of the beast. Now it divides where where it says

"shall drink of the wine of the wrath of God," for more insight turn to: Psalms 75:8 Isaiah 51:17 Jeremiah 25:15 Now Psalms 75:8

"For in the hand of the Lord there is a cup, and the wine is red; it is full of mixture, and he poureth out of the same: but the dregs thereof, all the wicked of the earth shall wring them out, and drink them." Now you know in the hand of the Lord there is a cup, and in that cup is red wine; it is full of mixture, so the people that worship the image of the beast and receive his mark in his forehead, or in his hand.

13

"The same shall drink of the wine of the wrath of God, which is poured out without mixture into the cup of his indignation;"

Isaiah 51:17

"Awake, awake, stand up, O Jerusalem, which hast drink at the hand of the LORD the cup of his fury; thou hast drunken the dregs of the cup of trembling, and wrung them out." Now Jerusalem shall drink at the hand of the Lord the cup of his fury because God said and I will punish the world for their evil,

Jeremiah 25:15

"For thus saith the LORD God of Israel unto me; Take the wine-cup of this fury at my hand, and cause all the nations, to whom I send thee, to drink it." Now God told Jeremiah to take the wine cup of of this fury at my hand and cause all the nations to whom God send Jeremiah to drink it, and they will drink it and the wrath of God will be on them. Now verse 16 says:

"And they shall drink, and be moved, and be mad, because of the sword that I will send among them." God will send the sword that is war among the nations. And this is what is starting to happen right now, war among the nations. Now back to Revelation 14:10 where it says:

"poured out without mixture into" Then it goes to Revelation 18:6

"Reward her even as she rewarded you, and double unto her double according to her works; in the cup which she hath filled, fill to her double." The Bible says to reward her even as she rewards you. That is that the Roman Catholic Church, the Vatican, the last pope that will come in is the false prophet that will bring war and destruction to many nations. She causes many to be killed; even the saints, and she shall get her reward even double because she hath shed the blood of the saints. Her reward will be poured out without mixture to punish her for her sins. And that false prophet deceived the people, which received the mark of the beast.

Now the next dividing is in Revelation 14:10 where it says: "the cup of his indignation;" let's go to Revelation 16:19 "And the great city was divided into three parts, and the cities of the nations fell: and great Babylon came in remembrance before God, to give unto her the cup of the wine of the fierceness of his wrath." Now the cup of the wine is the wrath of God. Babylon will be destroyed, that whorish system, with all of the false teachings in all of these churches teaching doctrine of men. Now the next dividing is in verse 10 where it says:

"he shall be tormented with" for better detail turn to Revelation 20:10

"And the devil that deceived them was cast into the lake of fire and brimstone, where the beast and the false prophet are, and shall be tormented day and night for ever and ever." Now everyone that worshiped the beast and his image and received the mark of the beast, shall be cast into the lake of fire and tormented day and night for ever and ever, "where the beast and the false prophet are," Now the next dividing in Revelation 14:10 where it says:

"fire and brimstone in the presence of the holy angels, and in the presence of the Lambs" let's turn to Revelation 19:20

"And the beast was taken, and with him the false prophet that wrought miracles before him, with which he deceived them that had received the mark of the beast, and them that worshiped his image. These both were cast alive into a lake of fire burning with brimstone." Now like I said earlier, the people that were deceived by that false prophet and had received the mark of the beast, and them that worshipped his image were both cast alive into a lake of fire burning with brimstone. I believe the mark of the beast is the computer chip in your right hand or in your forehead.

back to Revelation 14:11

"And the smoke of their torment ascendeth up for ever and ever: and they have no rest day nor night, who worship the beast and his image, and whosoever receiveth the mark of his name." You will feel yourself burning for ever and ever. Now it divides where it says: "the smoke of their torment ascendeth up for ever and ever." For more insight turn to Isaiah 34:10, then Revelation 19:3.

Isaiah 34:10

"It shall not be quenched night nor day; the smoke thereof shall go up for ever: from generation to generation it shall lie waste; none shall pass through it for ever and ever." Now that Babylonian system will burn day and night, all that worshipped the image of the beast and received his mark in their right hand or in their forehead, the smoke will go up forever.

Revelation 19:3

"And again they said, Alleluia. And her smoke rose up for ever and ever." Babylon will burn, and her smoke shall rise up for ever and ever.

Now back to Revelation 14:12

"Here is the patience of the saints: here are they that keep the commandments of God, and the faith of Jesus." Then it divides where it says, "Here is the patience of the saint." It goes to Revelation 13:10

"He that leadeth into captivity, shall go into captivity: he that killeth with the sword, must be killed with the sword. Here is the patience and the faith of the saints." In order to endure to the end, the saints must have patience because the great tribulation will be the worst time since there was a nation, and there never shall be a time like that. Now the next dividing in verse 12 where it says, "here are they that keep the commandments of God, and the faith of Jesus."

Revelation 12:17

"And the dragon was wroth with the woman, and went to make war with the remnant of her seed, which keep the commandments of God, and have the testimony of Jesus Christ."

The dragon was angry with the woman, the woman is the church, the true church, because she keep the commandments of God. The dragon was angry at the true church and that the time of the great tribulation.

Revelation 14:13

"And I heard a voice from heaven, saying unto me, write, Blessed are the dead which die in the Lord from henceforth: yea, saith the Spirit, that they may rest from their labours; and their works do follow them." It divides where it says. "Blessed are the dead." For more detail turn to Ecclesiastes 4:1,2 then Revelation 20:6.

Now Ecclesiastes 4:1.2

"So I returned, and considered all the oppressions that are done under the sun: and behold the tears of such as were oppressed, and they had no comforter; and on the side of their oppressors there was power; but they had no comforter." Now verse 2

"Wherefore I praised the dead which are already dead more than the living which are yet alive." Now the Bible says in verse 2, wherefore I praised the dead because the oppressors oppressed those that are living. Because in the time of great tribulation, the oppressors will oppress the saints of God and them that die in the Lord are blessed.

Revelation 20:6

"Blessed and holy is he that hath part in the first resurrection: on such the second death hath no power, but they shall be priests of God and of Christ, and shall reign with him a thousand years." Now blessed are the ones that die in the Lord, and they will live and reign with Christ a thousand years. Back to Revelation 14:13 where it says, "which die in the Lord." It then goes to 1 Corinthians 15:18, 1 Thessalonians 4:16. Now 1 Corinthians 15:18, I will start with verse 17 so that you might understand.

"And if Christ be not raised, your faith is vain; ye are yet in your sins." If Christ be not raised, you are yet in your sins. Now verse 18

"Then they also which are fallen asleep in Christ are perished." You see, if Christ were not raised from the dead, they that are dead in Christ will rise not, so they will perish. But Christ is raised from the dead and He is alive forever more. So this is why the dead in Christ shall rise.

Now 1 Thessalonians 4:16

"For the Lord himself shall descend from heaven with a shout, with the voice of the archangel, and with the trump of God: and the dead in Christ shall rise first:" Now the dead in Christ shall rise first. Now verse 17 says:

"Then we which are alive and remain shall be caught up together with them in the clouds, to meet the Lord in the air: and so shall we ever be with the Lord." Now some of the saints will remain alive when Christ come in the clouds, but the dead in Christ shall rise first out of the grave. Then we will, all together, meet the Lord in the air when he is coming back down to earth, to Jerusalem; and we shall rule and shall reign with him a thousand years. "And so shall we ever be with the Lord."

Back to Revelation 14:13

"that they may rest from their labours; and their works do follow them." Let us turn to 2 Thessalonians 1:7, Hebrews 4:9,10, Revelation 6:11.

Now 2 Thessalonians 1:7

"And to you, who are troubled, rest with us, when the Lord Jesus shall be revealed from heaven with his mighty angels," the ones that died in the Lord, there is a place of rest for them.

Now Hebrews 4:9,10

"There remaineth therefore a rest to the people of God." Verse 10

"For he that is entered into his rest, he also hath ceased from his own works, as God did from his.)" Now if we believed in Christ, and keep his commandment, and endure unto the end, shall enter into his rest.

Revelation 6:11

"And white robes were given unto every one of them; and it was said unto them, that they should rest yet for a little season, until their fellow servants also and their brethren, that should be killed as they were, should be fulfilled." Now the ones that died in the Lord, entered into his rest.

Now back to Revelation 14:14

"And I looked, and behold, a white cloud, and upon the cloud one sat like unto the Son of man, having on his head a golden crown, and in his hand a sharp sickle." It divides where it says, "like unto the Son of man," Now the son of man is the Lord Jesus Christ.

It goes to Ezekiel 1:26, Daniel 7:13, and Revelation 1:13. Now Ezekiel 1:26

"And above the firmament that was over their heads was the likeness of a throne, as the appearance of a sapphire stone: and upon the likeness of the throne was the likeness as the appearance of a man above upon it." Now the throne was the likeness as the appearance of a man above upon it. That man was the Lord Jesus Christ.

Daniel 7:13

"I saw in the night visions, and behold, one like the Son of man came with the clouds of heaven, and come to the ancient of days, and they brought him near before him." One like the Son of man is Jesus Christ that is coming immediately after the tribulation of those days after Babylon is destroyed.

Revelation 1:13

"And in the midst of the seven candlesticks one like unto the Son of man, clothed with a garment down to the foot, and girt about the paps with a golden girdle." Now the seven candlesticks are the seven churches. Now one like unto the Son of man is the Lord Jesus Christ, and the world were created by him.

Revelation 14:14 where it says, "having on his head a golden crown," for better detail to Revelation 6:2

"And I saw, and behold, a white horse: and he that sat on him had a bow; and a crown was given unto him: and he went forth conquering, and to conquer." Now some of these preachers, teachers, and false prophets say that the one on the white horse in Revelation 6:2 is the pope of Rome, the head of the Catholic Church. But that is not true, the rider on the white horse in Revelation 6:2 is Jesus Christ. White represents purity, but you never read anywhere in the Bible where the fallen angels sat on a white horse or any horse. You only read about the Lord Jesus Christ on a horse, and his angels. Now some of these preachers, teachers, and false prophets say that this rider had a bow, but no arrow. But the truth is, the bow and the arrow go together, and God uses them.

Turn to Lamentations 2:4

"He hath bent his bow like an enemy: he stood with his right hand as an adversary and slew all that were pleasant to the eye in the tabernacle of the daughter of Zion: he poured out his fury like fire." Now you see, the Lord bent his bow to destroy his people in the first Babylon. And he destroyed many of them because they had sinned against the Lord, and he will do the same thing in this Babylon. I believe that the first seal was opened on September 11, 2001 when president Bush went to war with Iraq and that is when the first trumpet sounded. Hail and fire mingled with blood because when we have stormy weather, we have hail in the land. And when summer and fall gets here, we have fire in the land, and now we are having war, bloodshed. Hail and fire mingled with blood, and this is what we are seeing now. Now back to the bow and arrow.

Turn to Psalms 7:11,12,13

"God judgeth the righteous, and God is angry with the wicked everyday."

Verse 12

"If he turn not, he will whet his sword; he hath bent his bow, and made it ready." Now you see, the Lord bent his bow and made it ready for war, just like he did in Revelation chapter 6. When he opened the first seal, he bent his bow for war to destroy the wicked and the sinners.

Verse 13

"He hath also prepared for him the instruments of death; he ordaineth his arrows against the persecutors." Now verse 13 says, God ordaineth his arrows against the persecutors. Now you read he uses arrows and the bow. The arrows and bow go together to kill and destroy with the sword for war. Now Revelation 6:2 where it says, "and a crown was given unto him:" So the false preachers, teachers, and prophets says this rider on the white horse had one crown. And the one in Revelation 19:12, had many crowns, so they say that is not the same rider. So they say the one in Revelation chapter 6 only had one crown, so they say that is thee antichrist, but that is not true. The rider in Revelation 6:2, and. the one in Revelation 14:14, and Revelation 19:12 are the same one, the Lord Jesus Christ. Now in chapter 6 and chapter 14 of Revelation, he had only one crown. So now I will try to explain to you what this means. Now in Revelation 6:2, it divides where it says, "And a crown was given unto him:" for more detail turn to Zechariah 6:11 and Revelation 14:14.

Now Zechariah 6:11

"Then take silver and gold, and make crowns, and set them upon the head of Joshua the son of Josedech, the high priest;" Now the one who made the crown took silver and gold to make the crowns. Now the word crown has an "S" on the word crown. One crown was made of many little crowns, around on top of that one big crown. Now the many crowns you read about, that Jesus Christ had on his head, is one crown.

In Revelation 19:12, I hope that you might understand, but I will explain it to you. Jesus Christ is the high priest now, and he has a crown on his head.

Now back to Revelation 14:15

"And another angel came out of the temple, crying with a loud voice to him that sat on the cloud, Thrust in thy sickle, and reap: for the time is come for thee to reap; for the harvest of the earth is ripe." It then divides where it says, "came out of the temple, crying with a loud voice to him that sat on the cloud,"

It goes to Revelation 16:17

"And the seventh angel poured out his vial into the air; there came a great voice out of the temple of heaven, from the throne, saying. It is done." Now the great voice out of the temple of heaven from the throne. Saying, it is done. Now I believe that is Jesus Christ. Now the next dividing is in verse 15 where it says, "Thrust in thy sickle, and reap: for the time is come for thee to reap; " Let's go to Joel 3:13, the Matthew 13:39.

Now Joel 3:13

"Put ye in the sickle, for the harvest is ripe: come, get you down; for the press is full, the fate overflow; for their wickedness is great." Now that will be the time of the battle of Armageddon. The Lord will gather the nations, the "multitudes, multitudes in the valley of decision:" to destroy them because of their wickedness. So the harvest of the earth is ripe.

Now Matthew 13:39

"The enemy that sowed them is the devil; the harvest is the end of the world; and the reapers are the angels." So the harvest is the end of the world, and that means that the world is ripe. Now the next dividing is in verse 15 where it says, "of the earth is ripe." It goes to Jeremiah 51:33, then Revelation 13:12.

Jeremiah 51:33

"For thus saith the LORD of hosts, the God of Israel; The daughter of Babylon is like a threshing-floor, it is time to thresh her: yet a little while, and the time of her harvest shall come." Now in the New Testament, when the second beast comes in, that means the earth is ripe. It is time for the harvest in a little while, meaning the iniquity has come to the full.

Revelation 13:12

"And he exerciseth all the power of the first beast before him, and causeth the earth and them which dwell there in to worship the first beast, whose deadly wound was healed." Now when the second beast come in, he will cause the people to worship the first, and the people won't be worshipping God. Now after he set up that image, he will only have three and a half years left, and then Babylon will be destroyed.

Revelation 14:16

"And he that sat on the cloud thrust in his sickle on the earth; and the earth was reaped." So that was Jesus Christ that sat on the cloud, he thrust in his sickle on the earth; and the earth was reaped.

Now verse 17

"And another angel came out of the temple which is in heaven, he also having a sharp sickle."

Verse 18

"And another angel came out from the altar, which had power over fire; and cried with a loud cry to him that had the sharp sickle, saying, Thrust in thy sharp sickle, and gather the clusters of the vine of the earth; for her grapes are fully ripe." It divides where it says, "which had power over fire."

For more insight turn to Revelation 16:8

"And the fourth angel poured out his vial upon the sun; and power was given unto him to scorch men with fire." The fourth angel had power over fire to scorch men upon the earth, and men will blasphemed the name of God because of the heat. Now the next dividing is in verse 18 where it says. "Thrust in thy sharp sickle, and gather clusters of the vine of the earth; for her grapes are fully ripe."

Joel 3:13

"Put ye in the sickle, for the harvest is ripe: come, get you down; for the press is full, the fats overflow; for their wickedness is great." Now when thee antichrist comes in, the iniquity has come to its full for the harvest is ripe: because the wickedness is great in the earth.

Back to Revelation 14:19

"And the angel thrust in his sickle into the earth, and gathered the vine of the earth, and cast it into the great wine-press of the wrath of God."

It divides where it says, "the great wine-press of the wrath of God." Revelation 19:15

"And out of his mouth goeth a sharp sword, that with it he should smite the nations: and he shall rule them with a rod of iron: and he treadeth the wine-press of the fierceness and wrath of Almighty God." So he punished those nations, he destroyed many people because the wickedness of their doing. The Lord was clothed with vesture dipped in blood.

Now Revelation 14:20

"And the wine-press was trodden without the city, and blood came out of the winepress, even unto the horse-bridles, by the space of a thousand and six hundred furlongs." It then divides where it says, "the winepress was trodden." Now let's turn to Isaiah 63:3, then Lamentations 1:15.

Isaiah 63:3

"I have trodden the winepress alone; and of the people there was none with me: for I will tread them in mine anger, and trample them in my fury; and their blood shall be sprinkled upon my garments, and I will stain all my raiment." The Lord alone will destroy that Babylonia system. That whore church and all of the rest of the false churches, which teaches false doctrine, and the ten horns armies, and the false prophet will be destroyed.

Lamentations 1:15

"The Lord hath trodden under foot all my mighty men in the midst of me: he hath call an assembly against me to crush my young men: the Lord hath trodden the virgin, the daughter of Judah, as in a winepress." The Lord will destroy the mighty men. He will trodden then under foot, as in a wine-press, many shall be destroyed. Now the next dividing is in verse 20 where it says, "without the city, and blood came out of the wine-press." For more information turn to Revelation 11:8, then Hebrews 13:12.

Revelation 11:8

"And their dead bodies shall lie in the street of the great city, which spiritually is called Sodom and Egypt, where also our Lord was crucified." They will kill the two witnesses, right outside of the city. In that period of time, Jerusalem shall go into captivity for three and a half years. In Jerusalem, some will be killed, and some will go into captivity into all nations.

Hebrews 13:12

"Wherefore Jesus also, that he might sanctify the people with his own blood, suffered without the gate." Jesus was crucified outside the gate, outside the city. Even the battle of Armageddon will be outside of Jerusalem. It will be bloodshed round about Jerusalem. Now the next dividing is in verse 20 where it says, "even unto the horse-bridles, by the space of a thousand and six hundred furlongs."

Revelation 19:14

"And the armies which were in heaven followed him upon white horses, clothed in fine linen, white and clean." Many will be killed, and this is God's doing, and his armies will be with him upon white horses. White stand for purity.

Revelation 9:1

"And the fifth angel sounded, and I saw a star fall from heaven unto the earth: and to him was given the key of the bottomless pit." the angel was given the key of the bottomless pit, to let satan out. Now it divides where it says, "And I saw a star fall from heaven unto the earth" Let's go to Luke 10:18 and Revelation 8:10.

Luke 10:18

"And he said unto them, I beheld Satan as lightning fall from heaven." Now Satan is falling and he is coming down unto us.

Revelation 8:10

"And the third angel sounded, and there fell a great star from heaven, burning as it were a lamp, and it fell upon the third part of the rivers, and upon the fountain of waters;" A star is an angel, and it fell upon the rivers and upon the fountain of waters. Now the next dividing is in verse 1 where it says, "the bottomless pit." It goes to:

Luke 8:31

Revelation 17:8

Revelation 20:1 Revelation 9:2,11

Luke 8:31

"And they besought him that he would not command them to go out into the deep." You see, these evil spirits ask Jesus not to command them, to go into the bottomless pit. Like I said before, the antichrist comes in the fifth trumpet. Now these other kings, beast come in before the antichrist the false prophet. The false prophet comes in last. The second beast in Revelation 13:11, and the fourth beast in Daniel 7:7,8.

Now back to Revelation 17:8

"The beast that thou sawest, was, and is not; and shall ascend out of the bottomless pit, and go into perdition: and they that dwell on the earth shall wonder, (whose names were not written in the book of life from the foundation of the world,) when they behold the beast that was, and is not, and yet is." You see, the fourth beast came out of the bottomless pit. The second beast in Revelation show's that a beast kill and destroys.

Revelation 20:1

"And I saw an angel come down from heaven, having the key of the bottomless pit and a great chain in his hand." The angel that comes down from heaven having the key of the bottomless pit is the Lord Jesus Christ and a great chain in his hand to lock Satan up for a thousand years.

Now Revelation 9:2

"And he opened the bottomless pit; and there arose a smoke out of the pit, as the smoke of a great furnace; and the sun and the air were darkened by reason of the smoke of the pit." He opened the bottomless pit.

Verse 11

"And they had a king over them, which is the angel of the bottomless pit, whose name in the Hebrew tongue is Abaddon, but in the Greek tongue hath his name Apollyn." Satan is the angel of the bottomless pit. He will get into that false prophet, and that false prophet will reign over the kings of the earth from that catholic church.

Revelation 9:2

"And he opened the bottomless pit; and there arose a smoke out of the pit, as the smoke of a great furnace; and the sun and the air were darkened by reason of the smoke of the pit." Now it divides where it says, "And there arose a smoke out of the pit," for more detail turn to Joel 2:2,10. Verse 2

"A day of darkness and of gloominess, a day of clouds and of thick darkness, as the morning spread upon the mountains: a great people and a strong; there hath not been ever the like, neither shall be any more after it, even to the years of many generations." And that is when Satan will come down onto us, having great wrath. That is also when the great tribulation starts, and that is when Satan will get into that false prophet. That false prophet will get with the ten kings, and they will receive power as kings one hour with the beast, the false prophet.

Joel 2:10

"The earth shall quake before them; the heavens shall tremble: the sun and the moon shall be dark, and the stars shall withdraw their shining:" That when the little horn, the false prophet, get with the ten kings, then he shall work deceitfully.

Revelation 9:3

"And there came out of the smoke locusts upon the earth: and unto them was given power, as the scorpions of the earth have power." Now there came out of the smoke locusts upon the earth, which means the ten kings armies. You see, unto them was given power, so that when the ten kings receive power as kings one hour with the beast, the false prophet. Now it divides in verse 3 where it says, "locusts upon the earth:" Let us now turn to Exodus 10:4, then Judges 7:12.

Exodus 10:4

"Else, if thou refuse to let my people go, behold, to-morrow will I bring the locusts into thy coast:" Now this is the natural locusts, like a grasshopper who God sent on the Egyptians.

Judges 7:12

"And the Midianites, and the Amalekites, and all the children of the east, lay along in the valley like grasshoppers for multitude; and their camels were without number, as the sand by the seaside for multitude." The locusts upon the earth are that of a great army, the ten kings armies, and the antichrist is the false prophet, the head of them. Now the next dividing is in Revelation 9:3 where it says, "as the scorpions of the earth have power." Fore better detail turn to verse 10

"And they had tails like unto scorpions, and there were stings in their tails: and their power was to hurt men five months." You see, "as the scorpions of the earth have power", that means that the ten kings received power from the beast, the false prophet which is in Revelation 17:12.

Revelation 17:12

"And the ten horns which thou sawest are ten kings, which have received no kingdom as yet; but receive power as kings one hour with the beast." The ten kings will receive power as the scorpions of the earth have power, and they had tails like scorpions. They had tails means they had false prophets. The tails are the false prophets, which cause the people to be hurt and destroyed. Verse 4:

"And it was commanded them that they should not hurt the grass of the earth, neither any green thing, neither any tree; but only those men which have not the seal of God in their foreheads." So it was commanded that the army should not hurt the grass of the earth, neither any green thing nor tree; but only those men which have not the seal of God in their foreheads. Now it divides where it says, "that they should not hurt". Let us turn to Revelation 6:6, then Revelation 7:3.

Revelation 6:6

"And I heard a voice in the midst of the four beasts say, a measure of wheat for a penny, and three measure of barley for a penny; and see thou hurt not the oil and the wine." Now in this verse the oil and the wine will not be hurt.

Revelation 7:3

"Saying, hurt not the earth, neither the sea, nor the trees, till we have sealed the servants of our God in their foreheads." You see, the other angel told the four angels not to hurt the earth, neither the sea, nor the trees, until we have sealed the servants of our God in their foreheads. Now the nest dividing is in verse 4 where it says, "the grass of the earth, neither any green thing, neither any tree;"

Revelation 8:7

"The first angel sounded and there followed hail and fire mingled with blood, and they were cast upon the earth: and the third part of trees was burnt up, and all green grass was burnt up." In the first trumpet, the third part of the trees was burnt up, and all green grass was burnt up. But in Revelation 9:4, that army was commanded not to hurt the grass and the trees of the earth, "but only those men which have not the seal of God in their foreheads." Now the next dividing is in verse 4 where it says, "the seal of God in their foreheads." For more insight turn to Revelation 7:3, Exodus 12:23, and Ezekiel 9:4. Now in Revelation 7:3

"Saying, Hurt not the earth, neither the sea, nor the trees, till we have sealed the servants of our God in their foreheads." It won't hurt God's people because they are sealed.

Exodus 12:23

"For the LORD will pass through to smite the Egyptians; and when he seeth the blood upon the lintel, and on the two side-posts, the LORD will pass over the door, and will not suffer the destroyer to come in unto your houses to smite you." The Israelite were seal because they obeyed the Lord by putting the blood upon the lintel and on the two side-posts.

Now Ezekiel 9:4

"And the LORD said unto him, Go through the midst of the city, through the midst of Jerusalem, and set a mark upon the foreheads of the men that sigh and that cry for all the abominations that be done in the midst thereof." God will set a mark upon his people, whatever that will be, and that will hurt men for five months. It will probably be some kind of plague. God's people will not get hurt by that plague. It will only hurt the unrighteous.

Revelation 9:5

"And to them it was given that they should not kill them, but that they should be tormented five months: and their torment was as the torment of a scorpion, when he striketh a man." Men will be tormented for five months. Now it divides where it says, "but that they should be tormented five months:" It goes to verse 10, "And they had tails like unto scorpions, and there were stings in their tails: and their power was to hurt men five months." They had tails like scorpions, and now the tails are the false prophets.

Revelation 9:6

"And in those days shall men seek death, and shall not find it; and shall desire to die, and death shall flee from them." At that time men shall seek death. Now it divides where it says, "shall men seek death, and shall not fine it;" For more detail turn to:

Job 3:21

Isaiah 2:19

Jeremiah 8:3

Revelation 6:16

Job 3:21

"Which long for death, but it cometh not; and dig for it more than for hid treasures;" Men will be tormented for five months, and they will want to die because of their pain and because they don't want to repent.

Isaiah 2:19

"And they shall go into the holes of the rocks, and into the caves of the earth, for fear of the LORD, and for the glory of his majesty, when he ariseth to shake terribly the earth." You see, men will be seeking death because he doesn't want to repent.

Jeremiah 8:3

"And death shall be chosen rather than life by all the residue of them that remain of this evil family, which remain in all the places whither I have driven them, saith the LORD of hosts." Men have chosen death because he doesn't want to repent from his sins. God shall destroy him because he doesn't want to repent from his sins so he is seeking death.

Revelation 6:16

"And said to the mountains and rocks, Fall on us, and hide us from the face of him that sitteth on the throne, and from the wrath of the Lamb:" Men shall be seeking death because he want the mountains and rocks to fall on them. And they don't want to repent, so they shall seek death.

Revelation 9:7

"And the shapes of the locusts were like unto horses prepared unto battle; and on their heads were as it were crowns like gold, and their faces were as the faces of men." The locusts are airplanes, and men are riding in them. They put on helmets before they start flinging the airplanes, and you only see their faces, so their faces were as men. It divides where it says, "the shapes of the locusts were like unto horses prepared unto battle;" For better understanding turn to Joel 2:4 where it is the same thing in Revelation chapter 9, as in Joel 2:4 where it reads:

"The appearance of them is as the appearance of horses; and as horsemen so shall they run." The horses are airplanes, and the horsemen are men in the airplanes. Now you read verse 5:

"Like the noise of chariots on the tops of mountains shall they leap, like the noise of a flame of fire that devoureth the stubble, as a strong people set in battle-array." Horses do not leap from tops of mountains. Now airplanes leap from the tops of mountains, and that's what it is, airplanes and people in them, a strong people. This is the same thing you read about in Revelation chapter 9. The Bible just talk about it in different ways, that's all, but it is the same event, the same thing. The little horn is the false prophet, the antichrist. Now the next dividing is in Revelation 9:7 where it says, "and on their heads were as it were crowns like gold," For more detail turn to Nahum 3:17. To fly those airplanes, those men put on a helmet.

Now Nahum 3:17

"Thy crowned are as the locusts, and thy captains as the great grasshoppers, which camp in the hedges in the cold day, but when the sun ariseth they flee away, and their place is not known where they are." The crown on the men heads is as the airplanes. Now the next dividing is in Revelation 9:7 where it says, "and their faces were as the faces of men." They were men in these planes, now the locusts are the airplanes and men are flying them, so they had the faces of men. For more insight, turn to Daniel 7:8.

Now Daniel 7:8

"I considered the horns, and behold there came up among them another little horn, before whom there were three of the first horns plucked up by the roots: and behold in this horn were eyes like the eyes of man, and a mouth speaking great things." This antichrist, the man of sin will see, things through the satellite by the computer. So he will have eyes like the eyes of men.

Now Revelation 9:8

"And they had hair as the hair of women, and their teeth were as the teeth of lions." It divides where it says, "their teeth were as the teeth of lions." Now they have hair like the hair of women because nowadays women fly airplanes. This is what John was seeing in heaven. He was seeing what was going to happen in the last days. For more insight to Joel 1:6.

Joel 1:6

"For a nation is come upon my land, strong, and without number, whose teeth are the teeth of a lion, and he hath the cheek teeth of a great lion." That is the ten horns army. I believe the ten horns, the ten kings, shall arise. The little horn is among them, the false prophet.

Revelation 9:9

"And they had breast-plates, as it were breast-plates of iron; and the sound of their wings was as the sound of chariots of many horses running to battle." They had breast-plates when the men and women set in these airplanes; the breastplates of the airplane surround them. God was showing John what is going to happen at the end time so John was explaining what he saw. In John's time they had chariots and horses; so now we replace chariots and horses with airplanes and helicopters, drone and tanks. John said they made sound like chariots and horses, and they had wings; horses do not have wings. Airplanes make sound when they take off, run and fly and airplanes have wings. This is how we fight war now, not with chariots and horses, but with airplanes, helicopters and tanks. This is what you are reading about in Revelation chapter 9. Now it divides in verse 9 where it says, "as the sound of chariots of many horses running to battle." For better detail turn to Joel 2:5,6,7.

Joel 2:5,6,7

"Like the noise of chariots on the tops of mountains shall they leap, like the noise of a flame of fire that devoureth the stubble, as a strong people set in battle-array." Like I said before, horses do not leap over mountains, but planes leaps over mountains. It makes noise of a flame of fire. Airplanes make noise, and it shut its missiles and makes fire and burn up things. The Bible says a strong people set in battle-array; there are people in these airplanes.

Verse 6

"Before their face the people shall be much pained: all faces shall gather blackness." When that army comes, these ten horns, ten kings army come, the people shall be in pain: that mean suffering, Round about that time, the great tribulation starts.

Verse 7

"They shall run like mighty men; they shall climb the wall like men of war; and they shall march every one on his ways, and they shall not break their ranks:" These mighty men, these line of soldiers, shall climb the wall like men of war.

Revelation 9:10

"And they had tails like unto scorpions, and there were stings in their tails: and their power was to hurt men five months." Now they had tails like unto scorpions, the tails are the false prophets. The false prophets cause the men to be hurt for five months. Now it divides where it says, "And their power was to hurt men five months."

Verse 5

"And to them it was given that they should not kill them, but that they should be tormented five months: and their torment was as the torment of a scorpions, when he striketh a man." The false prophets cause them to be tormented for five months. By teaching false doctrine, it leads to war.

Revelation 9:11

"And they had a king over them, which is the angel of the bottomless pit, whose name in the Hebrew tongue Abaddon, but in the Greek tongue hath his name Apollyon." You see they had a king over them, an army, and the false prophets. They worshipped Satan, the dragon; they had

Satan over them, "they worshipped the dragon which gave power unto the beast: and they worshipped the beast,"

Now it divides in Revelation 9:11 where it says, "And they had a king over them,"

Now turn to Ephesians 2:2

"Wherein in time past ye walked according to the course of this world, according to the prince of the power of the air, the spirit that now worketh in the children of disobedience:" These men had the spirit of disobedience in them, the spirit of Satan in them. The army, false prophets, and the people did not obey God. The next dividing is in verse 11 where it says, "the angel of the bottomless pit," It goes to verse 1:

"And the fifth angel sounded, and I saw a star fall from heaven unto the earth: and to him was given the key of the bottomless pit." The angel was given the key of the bottomless pit, and he opened the bottomless pit;

Revelation 9:12

"One woe is past; and behold, there come two woes more hereafter." Now the fifth trumpet has past, so now there are two more trumpets to sound. For more insight turn to Revelation 8:13.

Revelation 8:13

"And I beheld, and heard an angel flying through the midst of heaven, saying with a loud voice, Wo, wo, wo, to the inhabiters of the earth, by reason of the other voices of the trumpet of the three angels, which are yet to sound!" The voices of the trumpet are the seven angels, which had the seven trumpets, are the seven thunders that uttered their voices. Verse 13

"And the sixth angel sounded, and I heard a voice from the four horns of the golden altar which is before God," Verse 14

"Saying to the sixth angel which had the trumpet, loose the four angels which are bound in the great river Euphrates." Now these four angels were loose, which were bound in the great river Euphrates. Now it divides where it says, "in the great river Euphrates." Now turn to Revelation 16:12.

Revelation 16:12

"And the sixth angel poured out his vial upon the great river Euphrates; and the water thereof was dried up, that the way of the kings of the east might be prepared." Now the Euphrates River was dried up, that the kings of the east might be prepared for the battle of Armageddon. Verse 15

"And the four angels were loosed, which were prepared for an hour, and a day, and a month, and a year, for to slay the third part of men." These four angels were loosed to slay a third part of men in that army. Verse 16

"And the number of the army of the horsemen were two hundred thousand thousand and I heard the number of them." It divides where it says, "the number of the army." Now this is the number of the angels. For more insight turn to Psalms 68:17, then to Daniel 7:10.

Psalms 68:17

The chariots of God are twenty thousand, even thousands of angels: the Lord is among them, as in Sinai, in the holy place." The number of the army is God's angel.

Daniel 7:10

"A fiery stream issued and came forth from before him: thousand thousands ministered unto him, and ten thousand times ten thousand stood before him: the judgment was set, and the books were opened." Now the word, "books", with an "S" on it, is for the wicked. The books were opened to judge the wicked, the sinner, and that is the battle of Armageddon. This is what you read about in Revelation 9:16 and chapter 19. This is all the same battle in Joel chapter 3 and Ezekiel chapters 38 and 39. These chapters also state that the Lord will judge and destroy the wicked. The next dividing is in Revelation chapters 9 and 16 where it says, "of the horsemen were two hundred thousand thousand:" For more insight first turn to Enekiel 38:4.

Ezekiel 38:4

"And I will turn thee back, and put hooks into thy jaws, and I will bring thee forth, and all thine army, horses and horsemen, all of them clothed with all sorts of armour, even a great company with bucklers and shields, all of them handling swords:" That is when the Lord gathered all nations together, to battle, so that they might kill one another in the battle of Armageddon. The next dividing is where it says, "and I heard the number of them." For more information turn to Revelation 7:4.

Revelation 714

"And I heard the number of them which were sealed: and there were sealed a hundred and forty and four thousand of all the tribes of the children of Israel." John heard the number of them that were sealed; he did not see them that were sealed in this verse, but he just heard the number of them that were sealed.

Revelation 9:17

"And thus I saw the horses in the vision, and them that sat on them having breastplates of fire, and of jacinth, and brimstone: and the heads of the horses were as the heads of lions; and out of their mouth issued fire, and smoke, and brimstone." John said that he saw the horses in the vision. The horses are the airplanes, and them that sat on them are men. They sat in the airplanes and flew them. These men shut these missiles out of the airplane's mouth, and it issued fire, smoke, and brimstone. You see, now we fight with computer weapons. Then it divides says, "and the heads of the horses were as the heads of lions;" it goes to: 1 Chronicles 12:8 Isaiah 5:28,29

1 Chronicles 12:8

"And of the Gadites there separated themselves unto David into the hold to the wilderness men of might, and men of war fit for the battle, that could handle shield and buckler, whose faces were like the faces of lions, and were as swift as the roes upon the mountains;" This means that the army, the men of war, were strong as lions in Revelation 9:17

Isaiah 5:28

"Whose arrows are sharp, and all their bows bent, their horses hoofs shall be counted like flint, and their wheels like a whirlwind." Verse 29

"Their roaring shall be like a lion, they shall roar like young lions: yea, they shall roar, and lay hold of the prey, and shall carry it away safe, and none shall deliver it." They shall roar like young lions, which means that they are out to kill. They bent their bows for war to kill. Now Revelation 9:18

"By these three was the third part of men killed, by the fire, and by the smoke, and by the brimstone, which issued out of their mouths." This is what is going to happen in the battle of Armageddon. A third part of men shall be killed in that big army. Verse 19

"For their power is in their mouth, and in their tails: for their tails were like unto serpent, and had heads, and with them they do hurt." Their power is in their mouth, which is the missiles that come out from the airplanes, and their tails are the false prophets. Then it divides where it says, "for their tails were like unto serpents, and had heads," then it goes to:

Isaiah 9:15

"The ancient and honourable, he is the head; and the prophet that teacheth lies, he is the tail." The prophet that teaches lies is the tail, and he causes the people to be destroyed.

Now back to Revelation 9:21

"Neither repented they of their murders, nor of their sorceries, nor of their fornication, nor of their thefts." It divides where it says "nor of their sorceries, nor of their fornications, nor their thefts." For more insight turn to Revelation 22:15.

Revelation 22:15

"For without are dogs, and sorcerers, and whoremongers, and murderers, and idolaters, and whosoever loveth and maketh a lie." Now after all of these men were kill by the plagues, and the rest of the men which were not killed by the plagues, yet repented not. Neither of their murders, sorcerers, fornication, thefts, idolaters, "and whosoever loveth and maketh a lie"; and they will not inherit the kingdom of God.

Isaiah 9:16

"For the leaders of this people cause them to err; and they that are led of them are destroyed." The leaders of this people cause them to err, and that is the false prophet that causes the people to be destroyed that teaches lies. That is what you see in Revelation 9:17-19. That is what we see, many false prophets. False teaching causes people to be destroyed which leads to destruction.

Revelation 9:20

"And the rest of the men which were not killed by these plagues yet repented not of the works of their hands, that they should not worship devils, and idols of gold, and silver, and brass, and stone, and of wood: which neither can see, nor hear, nor walk:" After a third part of men were killed by these plagues, the rest of the men did not repent, and they kept on worshipping devils. It divides where it says, "yet repented not of the works of their hands," for better insight turn to:

Deuteronomy 31:29

"For I know that after my death ye will utterly corrupt yourselves, and turn aside from the way which I have commanded you; and evil will befall you in the latter days; because ye will do evil in the sight of the LORD, to provoke him to anger through the work of your hands." Now men are worshipping devils, with the work of their own hands. This is what is happening in the last days.

Revelation 10:1

"And I saw another mighty angel come down from heaven, clothed with a cloud: and a rainbow was upon his head, and his face was as it were the sun, and his feet as pillars of fire:" That mighty angel is the Lord Jesus Christ. And it divides where it says, "and a rainbow was upon his head," let's turn to Ezekiel 1:28.

Ezekiel 1:28

"As the appearance of the bow that is in the cloud in the day of rain, so was the appearance of the brightness round about. This was the appearance of the likeness of the glory of the LORD. And when I saw it, I fell upon my face, and I heard a voice of one that spake." Like I said before, that is Jesus Christ. The next dividing is where it says, "his face was as it were the sun," It goes to Matthew 17:2 and Revelation 1:16.

Matthew 17:2

"And was transfigured before them: and his face did shine as the sun, and his raiment was white as the light." That mighty angel in Revelation chapter 10 is Jesus Christ. The near dividing is where it says, "his feet as pillars of fire:" turn to Revelation 1:15.

Revelation 1:16

"And he had in his right hand seven stars: and out of his mouth went a sharp two-edged sword: and his countenance was as the sun shineth in his strength." The LORD face shine as the sun. He is not of darkness, but light.

Back to Revelation 10:2

"And he had in his hand a little book open: and he set his right foot upon the sea, and his left foot on the earth," That mean all power is given unto Jesus Christ, in heaven, and in earth. It divides where it says, "and he set his right foot upon the sea, and his left foot on the earth," For a better understanding, let's go to Matthew 28:18.

Matthew 28:18

"And Jesus came and spake unto them, saying, all power is given unto me in heaven and in earth." When Jesus put his right foot upon the sea and his left foot on the earth, which meant all power was given to him, in heaven and in the earth.

Back to Revelation 10:3

"And cried with a loud voice, as when a lion roareth: and when he had cried, seven thunders uttered their voices." When the Lord Jesus Christ cried with a loud voice, as when a lion roareth: and when he had cried, seven thunders uttered their voices. Now the seven thunders are the seven angels, which had the seven trumpets. This false prophet from South Carolina says the first thunder was when George Bush and Gorbachev met on the High Sea, on the Mediterranean Sea; that was the first thunder, but that is not true. He said the second thunder was when the Pope came to Denver, Colorado; but that is not true. He then says the third thunder was when the religious leaders came together in Chicago; but that is not true. He says the seven thunders were the voice of God; but that is the angels. The seven thunders were the voices of God, seven angels, which had seven trumpets. They have an "S" on the word "voice", so that mean there were more than one voice. So that means the seven thunders uttered their voices. The seven thunders are the seven angels, which had the seven trumpets. Now rightly dividing the word of truth where it says, "seven thunders uttered their voices". For better understanding turn to Revelation 8:5.

Revelation 8:5

"And the angel took the censer, and filled it with fire of the altar, and cast it into the earth: and there were voices, and thunderings, and lightnings, and an earthquake." There were voices, with an "S", and these were the seven angels, which had the seven trumpets. So now read on down in verse 6 and 7.

Verse 6

"And the seven angels which had the seven trumpets prepared themselves to sound." Now you see, the seven thunders are the seven angels, which had the seven trumpets, and they prepared themselves to sound.

Verse 7

"The first angel sounded and there followed hail and fire mingled with blood, and they were cast upon the earth: and the third part of trees was burnt up, and all green grass was burnt up." Now we are in the first trumpet. We have hail and fire mingled with blood, and it was cast upon the earth. When we have stormy weather, we have hail in the land; and then in the summer and fall, we have fire in the land upon earth. Now since 9/11, president Bush said there shall be war, and we have war now. That mean blood shed in the land, and upon the earth, and we have blood shed in the land. We have violent in the land like in the days of Noah. This is the first trumpet we see.

Revelation 10:4

"And when the seven thunders had uttered their voices, 1 was about to write: and I heard a voice from heaven saying unto me, seal up those things which the seven thunders uttered, and write them not." The Lord told John not to write the things, what the seven thunders uttered. He told John to seal up these things, which the seven thunders uttered, and write them not. Now later on, He told John to prophesy again in verse 11. "And he said unto me, Thou must prophesy again before many peoples, and nations, and tongues, and kings." Now you see, he told John to prophesy again. Now in Revelation 22:10 it says this, "And he saith unto me, Seal not the sayings of the prophecy of this book: for the time is at hand." Now you see, the Lord told John not to Seal the prophecy of this book. The prophecy of this book is not sealed. Now rightly dividing the word of truth.

Revelation 10:4

"Seal up those things which the seven thunders uttered, and write them not." Let's go to Daniel 8:26 and Daniel 12:4,9.

Daniel 8:26

"And the vision of the evening and the morning which was told is true: wherefore shut thou up the vision; for it shall be for many days." Now you see that the vision was sealed until the end of time.

Daniel 12:4

"But thou, O Daniel, shut up the words, and seal the book, even to the time of the end: many shall run to and fro, and knowledge shall be increased." You see the words of the book were sealed until the end of time and now we are at the end of time. The book is being opened up unto the righteous.

Daniel 12:9

"And he said, Go thy way, Daniel: for the words are closed up and sealed till the time of the end." The words were closed up until now. Now some of these preachers, teachers and prophets say that knowledge is increased for the unrighteous. But that is not true because the Bible says that they do not want to retain God in their knowledge. So knowledge has not increased for the ungodly. The righteous the Bible is talking about many shall run to and fro, and knowledge shall be increased; that mean increased for the righteous.

Revelation 10:5

"And the angel which I saw stand upon the sea and upon the earth, lifted up his hand to heaven," that was the Lord Jesus Christ. It divides where it says, "lifted up his hand to heaven." For more detail turn to Exodus 6:8 and Daniel 12:7.

Exodus 6:8

"And I will bring you in unto the land, concerning the which 1 did swear to give it to Abraham, to Isaac, and to Jacob; and I will give it you for an heritage: I am the LORD." Now when He lifted up his hand to heaven that mean that he swore by him that lives forever and ever.

Daniel 12:7

"And I heard the man clothed in linen, which was upon the waters of the river, when he held up his right hand and his left hand unto heaven, and sware by him that liveth for ever, that it shall be for a time, times, and a half; and when he shall have accomplished to scatter the power of the holy people, all these things shall be finished." You see, he lifted up his hands unto heaven and swore by him that live forever.

Back to Revelation 10:6

"And sware by him that liveth for ever and ever, who created heaven, and the things that therein are, and the earth, and the things that therein are, and the sea, and the things which are therein, that there should be time no longer:" Now it divides where it says "who created heaven, and the things that are," For a better understanding turn to Nehemiah 9:6, Revelation 4:11, and Revelation 14:7.

Now Nehemiah 9:6

"Thou, even thou, art LORD alone; thou hast made heaven, the heaven of heavens, with all their host, the earth, and all things that are therein, the seas, and all that is therein, and thou preservest them all; and the host of heaven worshippeth thee." There shall be time no longer for that beast system, the antichrist, the man of sin because God created all things.

Revelation 4:11

"Thou art worthy, O Lord, to receive glory, and honour, and power: for thou hast created all things, and for thy pleasure they are and were created." The Lord created all things for his pleasure.

Revelation 14:7

"Saying with a loud voice, Fear God, and give glory to him; for the hour of his judgment is come: and worship him that made heaven, and earth, and the sea, and the fountains of waters."

Revelation 10:7

"But in the days of the voice of the seventh angel, when he shall begin to sound, the mystery of God should be finished, as he hath declared to his servants the prophets." When the seventh trumpet sounds, it will last for days. I believe that's the last 45 days because it will be days after that great tribulation. Then the sun shall be darkening, and the moon shall not give her light, and that's when Jesus Christ is coming back.

Now it divides where it says in verse 7, "in the days of the voice of the seventh angel," turn to Revelation 11:15 for more insight.

Revelation 11:15

"And the seventh angel sounded; and there were great voices in heaven, saying. The kingdoms of this world are become *the kingdoms* of our Lord, and of his Christs; and he shall reign for ever and ever." Now after the sixth angel sounded and when the sixth trumpet finished, the seventh trumpet comes quickly. The great voices are the angels. Now let's go to Revelation 10:8.

Revelation 10:8

"And the voice which I heard from heaven spake unto me again, and said, Go, and take the little book which is open in the hand of the angel which standeth upon the sea and upon the earth." Now it divides where it says, "the voice which I heard from heaven spake unto me again and said, Go, and take the little book which is open in the hand of the angel which standeth upon the sea and upon the earth." The angel, whom stands upon the sea and upon the earth, is Jesus Christ. Let's run to Revelation 10:4.

Revelation 10:4

"And when the seven thunders had uttered their voices, I was about to write: And I heard a voice from heaven saying unto me, Seal up those things which the seven thunders uttered, and write them not." John heard a voice from heaven, that is the voice of God from heaven, and he told him to, "Seal up those things which the seven thunders uttered, and write them not."

Back to Revelation 109

"And I went unto the angel, and said unto him, give me the little book. And he said unto me, take it, and eat it up; and it shall make thy belly bitter, but it shall be in thy mouth sweet as honey." Then it divides where it says, "take it, and eat it up;" For more insight turn to: Jeremiah 15:16 Ezekiel 2:8 Ezekiel 3:1,2,3

Jeremiah 15:16

"Thy words were found, and I did eat them; and thy word was unto me the joy and rejoicing of mine heart: for I am called by thy name, O LORD God of hosts." Jeremiah did eat the words of the Lord; the word was in his heart.

Ezekiel 2:8

"But thou, son of man, hear what I say unto thee; Be not thou rebellious like that rebellious house: open thy mouth, and eat that 1 give thee." The Lord wanted Ezekiel to eat the words that he gives him.

Ezekiel 3:1

"Moreover he said unto me, Son of man, eat that thou findest; eat this roll, and go speak unto the house of Israel."

Ezekiel 3:2

"So I opened my mouth, and he caused me to eat that roll. Now you see that Ezekiel did eat the words of the Lord.

Ezekiel 3:3

"And he said unto me, Son of man, cause thy belly to eat, and fill thy bowels with this roll that I give thee. Then did I eat it; and it was in my mouth as honey for sweetness." Ezekiel did eat the words of the Lord, and spoke to the people the word of the Lord.

Now Revelation 10:10

"And I took the little book out of the angel's hand, and ate it up; and it was in my mouth sweet as honey: and as soon as I had eaten it my belly was bitter." The words of the Lord are sweet in the mouth of the Christian.

Revelation 10:11

"And he said unto me. Thou must prophesy again before many peoples, and nations, and tongues, and kings." So the Lord told John to prophesy again before many peoples, nations, tongues and kings. So the seven thunders are not sealed because the Lord told John not to seal the prophecy of this book in Revelation 22:10, and it says this: "And he saith unto me, Seal not the sayings of the prophecy of this book: for the time is at hand." You see the prophecy of this book is not sealed and one of the false prophets says that the first three thunders had already sounded. But that is not true; the seven thunders are the seven angels, which had the seven trumpets. We are in the first trumpet. We have hail fire mingled with blood in the world. When we have stormy weather, we have hail in the land. In the summer and fall, we have fire in the land, and since 9/11 we have war and violent bloodshed in the land, I will explain about the great tribulation and the two witnesses. The great tribulation starts after the two witnesses are killed because before Jerusalem are taken over by the Gentiles, God always sent his prophets to warn the people about their sins to repent or he will destroy them that sinned against him. In the New Testament he sent them by two or three, but in the Old Testament it was by one. If you read 1 Corinthians 14:29 says, "Let the prophets speak two or three, and let the other judge." You see in the New Testament the prophets speak two or three. So before Jerusalem is taken over, he will send the two witnesses. When the two witnesses finish their testimony, they will be killed and that is when the great tribulation starts. In the New Testament, the two witnesses and the saints are the daily sacrifice. I will talk about the daily sacrifices and the false prophet and many other things.

Revelation 11:7

"And when they shall have finished their testimony, the beast that ascendeth out of the bottomless pit shall make war against them, and shall overcome them, and kill them." It rightly divides the word of truth where it says, "shall have finished their testimony." For more insight, turn to Luke 13:32.

Luke 13:32

"And he said unto them, Go ye and tell that fox, Behold, I cast out devils, and I do cures to-day and to-morrow, and the third day I shall be perfected." The enemies of the two witnesses won't be able to do anything to them until they finish their testimony for three and a half years. Then they will be killed by their enemies. The next dividing is the word of truth, "the beast that ascendeth." For more insight turn to Revelation 13:1.

Revelation 13:1

"And I stood upon the sand of the sea, and saw a beast rise up out of the sea, having seven heads and ten horns, and upon his horns ten crowns, and upon his heads the name of blasphemy." These are the beast that are in Daniel, the world government, the lion, the bear, leopard, and the fourth beast. The fourth beast is the second beast in Revelation 13:11 where it says, "And I beheld another beast coming up out of the earth, and he had two horns like a lamb, and he spake as a dragon." This is false prophet, the antichrist. Now some people say the false prophet is not the antichrist. The false prophet is the antichrist. Anybody that is against Christ is an antichrist. Why are so many people so ignorant, and they cannot see that? The false prophet is telling the government what to do. You can read about the false prophet in Daniel 7:7,8,19-27, Daniel 8:9-12, 23-25, Daniel 11:21-45, Daniel 12:7-11 and 2 Thessalonians 2:3-10.

Now back to Revelation 11:7, where it divides the word of truth saying, "out of the bottomless pit." For a better understanding, turn to Revelation 9:2.

Revelation 9:2

"And he open the bottomless pit; and there arose a smoke out of the pit, as the smoke of a great furnace; and the sun and the air were darkened by reason of the smoke of the pit." That's when the antichrist showed up, the false prophet. Now back to Revelation 11:7, where it says, "Shall make war against them, and shall overcome them, and kill them." For more insight turn to Daniel 7:21 and Zechariah 14:2.

Daniel 7:21

"I beheld, and the same horn made war with the saints, and prevailed against them;" It is the antichrist that cause the two witnesses to be killed, which is the second beast in Revelation 13:11.

Now Zechariah 14:2 says: God said he will gather all nations against Jerusalem. That's the first time, and that's when the two witnesses will be killed, and they will set up the abomination that maketh desolate. That starts the great tribulation that will last three and a half years. Then God will gather all nations for the second time for the Battle of Armageddon. Some people think he will gather all nations one time, but it will be two times when he gathers all nations in the last days. The first time Jerusalem will be taking over and going into captivity; the second time, for the Battle of Armageddon.

Now I will read Zechariah 14:2

"For I will gather all nations against Jerusalem to battle; and the city shall be taken, and the houses rifled, and the women ravished; and half of the city shall go forth into captivity, and the residue of the people shall not be cut off from the city." You see Jerusalem shall be taking over by the Gentiles. But before it will be taken over of the Gentiles, God will send two witnesses just like in the first Babylon. God send Jeremiah to warn the people, before it was taken over. So Jerusalem will be taken over by the Gentiles for three and a half years, and then the Lord will go forth and fight against those nations, and that will be in the Battle Armageddon. You can read about it in Joel 3:2-17. In verse 2 he said, "I will also gather all nations, and will bring them down into the valley of Jehoshaphat," and that is the Battle of Armageddon. Then you can read about it in Zephaniah 3:8, "Therefore, wait ye upon me, saith the Lord, until the day that I rise up to the prey: for my determination is to gather the nations, that I may assemble the kingdoms, to pour upon them mine indignation, even all my fierce anger: for all the earth shall be devoured with the fire of my jealousy." This is the Battle of Armageddon in Ezekiel chapters 38 and 39, Revelation 9:13-21, Revelation 16:12-16, Revelation chapter 18 and Revelation 19:14-20. All of these chapters and verses are the Battle of

Armageddon, and it is also in Revelation 14:20. The Bible talk about it in different ways, but it is all the same battle, the Battle of Armageddon.

Now back to Daniel 7:21, and 1 would like to explain some things a little more. Daniel 7:21

"1 beheld, and the same horn made war with the saints, and prevailed against them;" then it rightly divides the word of truth where it says, "and the same horn made war with the saints, and prevailed against them;" for more information turn to Daniel 8:12-24, Daniel 11:31, Revelation 11:7, Revelation 13:7, Revelation 17:14, and Revelation 19:19.

Daniel 8:12

"And a host was given him against the daily sacrifice by reason of transgression, and it cast down the truth to the ground; and it practised, and prospered." You see an army was given to him against the daily sacrifice. The daily sacrifice is the saints and not animal sacrifice. Some of these false teachers, preachers, and prophets are saying that the daily sacrifice is animal sacrifice. That is not true. In the Old Testament, the daily sacrifice was the animal sacrifice. But in the New Testament, the daily sacrifices are the saints. When Christ died on the cross, animal sacrifice was done away with. So now the daily sacrifices are the saints. Daniel prophecy was for the future, for the end time. The daily sacrifices are the saints, read Romans 12:1, Hebrews 13:15 and 1 Peter 2:5. The saints are the daily sacrifices.

Daniel 8:24

"And his power shall be mighty, but not by his own power: and he shall destroy wonderfully, and shall prosper, and practice, and shall destroy the mighty and the holy people." He shall destroy the mighty and the holy people. The holy people are the saints so he will make war with the saints. He will not make war with animal sacrifice. The truth is not in animal sacrifice. The truth is in the saints, the Christians. That is who the antichrist will try to destroy, the saints.

Daniel 11:31

"And arms shall stand on his part, and they shall pollute the sanctuary of strength, and shall take away the daily sacrifice, and they shall place the abomination that maketh desolate." The Bible says they shall take away the daily sacrifice. That means that they will kill the saints, and put some in prison so they are taken away the daily sacrifice. This is what Jesus Christ talks about in Matthew 24:9, Mark 13:9 and Luke 21:12. Saul was doing this in Acts, persecuting the church and having them put in prison and some kill. Saul was taken away the daily sacrifice. Some of these false prophets, preachers, and teachers say when the Jew goes back to animal sacrifice. That will make the abomination that maketh desolate. These false prophets say that the antichrist will take away the animal sacrifice, and set up the abomination that maketh desolate. The animal sacrifice suppose to be the abomination that maketh desolate. It doesn't make sense. He is going to take away the abomination that maketh desolate, and set up the abomination that maketh desolate. He is going to take away the daily sacrifice because the daily sacrifices are the saints. He is going to make war with the saints. The daily sacrifice in the New Testament is not animal sacrifice. They are the saints of God in the New Testament. Come on people, put on your thinking cap when you read something, and put the pieces together. It suppose to make sense. The saints are the daily sacrifice.

Revelation 11:7

"And when they shall have finished their testimony, the beast that ascendeth out of the bottomless pit shall make war against them, and shall overcome them, and kill them." The beast is making war with the saints. He is not making war with animal. When he kills the two witnesses, Jerusalem will be taken over. That is when the great tribulation starts. You can read about the two witnesses in Psalm 79.

Palm 79

"O GOD, the heathen are come into thine inheritance; thy holy temple have they defiled; they have laid Jerusalem on heaps." That is when Jerusalem will be trodden under foot for three and a half years. Verse 2

"The dead bodies of thy servants have they given to be meat unto the fowls of the heaven, the flesh of thy saints unto the beasts of the earth." When they kill the two witnesses, they left their dead bodies for three and a half days in the street and not bury them. Verse 3

"Their blood have they shed like water round about Jerusalem; and there was none to bury them." They will shed the saints blood round about Jerusalem. They will kill the two witnesses, and kill some of those that are Christians because the antichrist will make war with the saints. Verse 4

"We are become a reproach to our neighbours, a scorn and derision to them that are round about us." All those nations around Israel hate Jesus and Christians. Verse 5

"How long, LORD? Wilt thou be angry for ever? Shall thy jealousy bum like fire?" It will be for three and a half years that great tribulation will last. Then he will gather all nations that came against Jerusalem in the Battle of Armageddon to destroy the wicked. Verse 6

"Pour out thy wrath upon the heathen that have not known thee, and upon the kingdoms that have not called upon thy name." God will pour out thy wrath upon the heathen that have not known him.

Revelation 13:7

"And it was given unto him to make war with the saints, and to overcome them: and power was given him over all kindreds, and tongues, and nations." He will make war with the saints, and kill the two witnesses. He will set up an image that will make the abomination that maketh desolate. He will want the whole world, all the nations, and people to worship the image of the beast. That will make the abomination of desolation. God said for you to not bow down yourself to any graven image. This is the second commandment. Some of these false prophets, preachers, and teaches say when Jews go back to sacrificing bulls goats that will make the abomination that maketh desolate. Bulls and goats are vanity. God is dealing with the whole world, not only just with the Jews. The antichrist will kill the two witnesses, and set up an image. That will make the abomination that maketh desolate, and that will start the great tribulation. After he kills the two witnesses, that is when the great tribulation starts for three and a half years. Some of these men say that the last forty five days are the great tribulation. That is not true; the great tribulation is three and a half years. If you read Matthew 24:29, "Immediately after the tribulation of those days, shall the sun be darkened, and the moon shall not give her light, and the stars shall fall from heaven, and the powers of the heavens shall be shaken:" The Lord said. "Immediately after the tribulation of those days," that means it will be days after the tribulation. Days with an "s" on it, the Lord will come back. That's the last forty five days, and that is the seventh trumpet. will talk about it a little later in Revelation 17:14.

Now Revelation 17:14

"These shall make war with the Lamb, and the Lamb shall overcome them; for he is Lord of lords, and Kings of kings; and they that are with him are called, and chosen, and faithful." The false prophet and the ten kings shall make war with the saints.

Now Revelation 19:19

"And I saw the beast, and the kings of the earth, and their armies, gathered together to make war against him that sat on the horse, and against his army." The beast, the false prophet, and the kings of the earth made war with Jesus Christ and the saints. Now let's go back to talking about the last forty five days.

Revelation 10:7

"But in the days of the voice of the seventh angel, when he shall begin to sound, the mystery of God should be finished, as he hath declared to his servants the prophets." The Bible say, "But in the days of the voice of the seventh angel", now you see how the Bible has an "s" on the word "days". The seventh trumpet will go on for days, and that is the last forty five days. The seventh trumpet is immediately after the tribulation. Now you can read about it in Daniel 12:11-12, and it says this:

"And from the time that the daily sacrifice shall be taken away, and the abomination that maketh desolate set up, there shall be a thousand two hundred and ninety days." So that's the time that they will kill the two witnesses and they will set up an image like Nebuchadnezzar did. That will make the abomination that maketh desolate, and that will be for three and a half years. Now verse 12

"Blessed is he that waiteth, and cometh to the thousand three hundred and five and thirty days." So that is forty five days more than the one thousand two hundred ninety days. The forty five days more is after the tribulation is over. That is when the sun shall be darkened, and the moon shall not give her light, and the stars shall fall from heaven. That will be in the last forty five days. You can read about it in the six seal, seventh trumpet, and in the seventh vial; that all come immediately after the tribulation of those days. Now let's go to Mark 13:24, it will give a clearer understanding. Now it says this, "But in those days, after that tribulation, the sun shall be darkened, and the moon shall not give her light, and the stars of heaven shall fall, and the powers that are in heaven shall be shaken. And then shall they see the Son of man coming in the clouds with great power and glory. And then shall he send his angels, and shall gather together his elect from the four winds from the uttermost part of the earth to the uttermost part of heaven." Now you see what the Bible says, but in those days after that tribulation. You see now it will be days after that tribulation, then Jesus Christ is coming back. That is the last forty five days after that tribulation, and then the Lord is coming back. Now there are so many false prophets, teachers and preachers nowadays. Just like the Lord said in Matthew chapter 24. Many will come in his name saying that he is Christ. He is Lord. And many were deceived because their teaching is false. He said "take heed that no man deceive you". Now I want to talk more about the daily sacrifice, and the abomination that maketh desolate. Now I will go back to Daniel 8:11-14. Verse 11

"Yea, he magnified himself even to the prince of the host, and by him the daily sacrifice was taken away, and the place of his sanctuary was cast down." You see he magnified himself. That means he declare himself as great, even to the prince of the host, Jesus Christ and the saints. "And by him the daily sacrifice was taken away," That means in the New Testament, he was killing the saints, and putting some in prison. The Lord sanctuary' was cast down and in Psalms chapter 79:1, the holy temple have they defiled. Verse 12

"And a host was given him against the daily sacrifice by reason transgression, and it cast down the truth to the ground; and in practiced, and prospered." It rightly divides the word of truth where it says, "a host was given him against the daily sacrifice by reason of transgression," now let's go to Daniel 11:31. That means an army was given to the antichrist against the two witnesses and the saints. Daniel 11:31

"And arms shall stand on his part, and they shall pollute the sanctuary of strength, and shall take away the daily sacrifice, and they shall place the abomination that maketh desolate." That is when they kill the two witnesses, and they shall place the abomination that maketh desolate. That is when the antichrist set up that image. You can read about it in Revelation 13:11-15. That is when the antichrist takes power in verse 11.

Revelation 13:14

"And deceiveth them that dwell on the earth by the means of those miracles which he had power to do in the sight of the beast; saying to them that dwell on the earth, that they should make an image to the beast, which had the wound by a sword, and did live." The false prophet is the second beast. He is the antichrist, and he said that they should make an image to the beast, which had the wound by a sword and did live. The antichrist told the people that they should make the image to the beast. That image will make the abomination that maketh desolate He said to make an image to the beast that had the wound by a sword, and did live. It was one of the first beast that got wounded, either the lion, bear, or the leopard. He probably got sick unto death or shot unto death, but he did live. Some people says it is Germany, the head that got wounded in world war II, and got healed when the Berlin wall came down. I believe that one of the leaders will get sick or shot unto death They will make an image unto that beast head that did live. The false prophet will want all people and nations to bow down and worship that image, or they should be killed. Verse 15

"And he had power to give life unto the image of the beast, that the image of the beast should both speak, and cause that as many as would not worship the image of the beast should be killed." Some of these false prophets and teachers say that the image of the beast is the apostate churches. But the truth is the image of the beast. It is an image, an idol that they will set up. Whosoever will not worship the image of the beast should be killed. I will read to you verse 16-18. Verse 16

"And he causeth all, both small and great, rich and poor, free and bond, to receive a mark in their right hand, or in their foreheads;" That is the computer chip probably in your right hand or in your forehead. Verse 17

"And that no man might buy or sell, save he that had the mark, or the name of the beast, or the number of his name." You see you won't be able to buy or sell except when you have the mark of the beast or the name of the beast or the number of his name. I believe the number of the beast is the card or other device, even a bar code. Verse 18

"Here is wisdom. let him that hath understanding count the number of the beast: for it is the number of a man; and his number is six hundred threescore and six." Now some people said that kissinger was the antichrist. Bill Clinton was the antichrist because their name turns out to be 666, by using the Roman numeral number, but that is not true. The Bible says to count the number of the beast so that beast government uses a number, he uses the number 666. For it is the number of a man so that means a man came out with that number to run that computer. That number did not come from God just like when God told Noah to make the ark three hundred cubits length.

Genesis 6:15

"And this is the fashion which thou shall make it of: The length of the ark shall be three hundred cubits, the breadth of it fifty cubits, and the height of it thirty cubits." You see this number came from God, but the number in Revelation 13:18, that number came from man. That is the number of a man. For more detail turn to Revelation 21:17, and it says this, "And he measured the wall thereof, a hundred and forty and four cubits according to the measure of a man, that is, of the angel." The angel measures the city according to the measure of a man. When you measure something, you come up with a number. So 666 is the number of a man. A man came out with that number, and that is the number the beast system use. We are coming to the final stage because the FDA had approved the computer chip implant in humans. I thank God his words is being fulfilled. I heard one prophet said that the computer chip would not be the mark of the beast. According to my understanding, I knew the computer chip would probably be the mark of the beast.

Now back to Daniel 8:12, "the truth to the ground;" He cast down the truth to the ground, that means he cast down God's laws. For a better understanding turn to Psalms 119:43,142, and then Isaiah 59:14.

Isaiah 59:14.

"And judgment is turn away backward, and justice standeth afar off: for truth is fallen in the street, and equity cannot enter." There is no justice in the land today. The preachers, teachers and prophets don't know the law of God anymore because truth is fallen in the street. Truth is not in the courthouse, and not in the churches because their light is just about out. When the iniquity has come to it full, the light has gone out, and that's when that antichrist comes in.

Psalms 119:43

"And take not the word of truth utterly out of my mouth; for I have hope in thy judgments." We cannot find truth anymore in the justice system, and in the churches. Truth is in the street. There are only a few that have the truth. The elect and they are in the street.

Psalms 119:142

"Thy righteousness is an everlasting righteousness, and thy law is the truth." The antichrist will cast down the truth, which is the law of God. The law of God is being cast down now. It started many years ago because of false preachers, teachers and false prophets saying that we are not under the law that is true. We are not under the law. If we obey and keep the Lord's commandments, then we are not under the law, but under grace. But if we keep not the Lord's commandments, then we are under the law, and not under grace. Like if we steal, kill, commit adultery, commit fornication, or be a homosexual, and keep doing it and do not repent for that sin, then we are under the law and not under grace. But if we are under the law, then we shall receive punishment. This is the word of the Lord. Now back to Daniel 8:12, where it says, "practiced and prospered", for more insight turn to verse 4 and chapter 11:28, 36. Verse 4

"I saw the ram pushing westward, and northward, and southward; so that no beasts might stand before him, neither was there any that could deliver out of his hand; but he did according to his will, and became great." What this means is that he shall do according to his will and become great. Now 11:28

"Then shall he return into his land with great riches; and his heart shall be against the holy covenant; and he shall do exploits, and return to his own land." He shall prosper and he shall become rich. Verse 36

"And the king shall do according to his will; and he shall exalt himself, and magnify himself above every god, and shall speak marvelous things against the God of gods, and shall prosper till the indignation be accomplished: for that that is determined shall be done." The Bible says that the antichrist will speak marvelous things against the God of gods, and shall prosper.

Daniel 8:13

"Then I heard one saints speaking, and another saint said unto that certain saint which spake, How long shall be the vision concerning the daily sacrifice, and the transgression of desolation, to give both the sanctuary and the host to be trodden under foot?" One saint is speaking, and another saint is the angel. Angels are called "saints" too. Then it goes to Daniel 4:3, 12:6, and 1 Peter 1:12. Now the daily sacrifice, and the transgression of desolation give both the sanctuary and the host to be trodden under foot. The churches are being polluted now. The host and the saints are starting to be persecuted now. Some are being thrown in prison, and some are going to be killed. Verse 14

"And he said unto me, unto two thousand and three hundred days then shall the sanctuary be cleansed." Now I have never heard a preacher, teacher or prophet explain verse 11 to 14 because they can't explain it because they think that the daily sacrifice is animal sacrifice. If you think that you can't explain it because it won't make sense, it's because they think that the daily sacrifice is a animal. I am sorry I have to repeat myself so many times, but I want to make sure that you understand that the daily sacrifice are the saints of God in the new covenant. The Bible says unto two thousand and three hundred days, and then shall the sanctuary be cleansed. The antichrist came in before he set up the abomination that make it desolate. He came in Daniel 11:21. The antichrist and league made with those ten kings, and he fought a war against the king of the south before he set up the abomination that maketh desolate. I believe the king of the south is Israel. In verse 31 he take away the daily sacrifice which is when he kills the two witnesses, saints and probably put some in prison. When the iniquity comes to its full that is when the antichrist came into power. You can read about it in Daniel 8:23. He came in before he set up the abomination that maketh desolate. That will last for three and a half years because the Bible says unto two thousand and three hundred days then shall the sanctuary be cleansed. That means from the time he took power until the time he was destroyed and Christ came back. That will probably be the two thousand three hundredth day. The people are in darkness because the prophets are in darkness. They don't know the law of God anymore, and the prophets are mad and arrogant. You can't talk to them or correct them when they are in error because they are like a mad dog. They are drunk with the wine of her fornication. There are two types of people, a mad and a drunken person. You can't tell them anything. The whole world is mad no matter what you say to these prophets. They will not listen because they are drunk and mad. They have drunk the wine of her fornication. They won't listen. God send them a strong delusion that they should believe a lie because they love not the truth. The prophets are against one another, and they steal God's words from their neighbors like on the internet and elsewhere. God is not speaking directly to them, like he did Moses and the other prophets. In Jeremiah 23:30 it says, "Therefore, behold, I am against the prophets, saith the LORD, that steal my words everyone from his neighbour." It is just like the false prophet from South Carolina, R. G. Stair. You see these false prophets steal God's words from their neighbors.. Verse 31

"Behold, I am against the prophets, saith the LORD, that use their tongues, and say, He saith." Then when you confront these false prophets about what they said before, they will say I didn't say that. But when you play back the tape, you find out that they said it; and you find out that they are liars. This is why they are mad and drunken with wine because they said things that was wrong. They interpret the scripture wrong, even the false prophet from South Carolina. At one time he say Rome is Babylon, and then next he will say the United States is Babylon. Now you see that he is confused. Then he will say the Pope is not the antichrist, and then next he will say that Bush is the antichrist. And then he says that the antichrist will be a political leader. But the truth is that the antichrist will be a false religious leader and a political leader. Just like Nebuchadnezzar, he rule over the religion and government, and the antichrist will do the same thing. Oh, the errors of the prophets. I will start in Matthew 24:28, "For wheresoever the carcass is, there will the eagles be gathered together." And I heard one prophet from South Carolina say that the verse means that the saints will be gathered together. He said this because the Bible says this in Isaiah 40:31, "But they that wait upon the Lord shall renew their strength; they shall mount up with wing as eagles; they shall run, and not be weary; and they shall walk, and not faint." Now this prophet from South Carolina says that what that means in Matthew 24:28 is what he is talking about. The Bible is talking about the saints in verse 28. But that is not true, but the Bible is talking about and it says this, "For wheresoever the carcass is, there will the eagles be gathered together." That means to eat the dead bodies like in the Battle of Armageddon. You will read about this in Ezekiel 39:17 and Revelation 19:17-18. I am trying to show God's people where the prophets are in error and that verse is in Matthew 24:28, and for more detail turn to Job 39:30, and it says this:

"Her young ones also suck up blood: and where the slain are, there is she." Now you see where the dead bodies are; there are the eagles. Now you can see where the prophets are in error, and the Battle of Armageddon come on the end of the great tribulation, and the lying prophet will say that I never said that because they are the love of money. The one from South Carolina will not admit that he was wrong. I will tell you about another error of the prophet.

Acts 2:45

"And sold their possessions and goods, and parted them to all men, as every man had need." Now you see that they sold their possessions and goods, and gave it to all men that were in need. The apostles didn't take the peoples' money for themselves or spend the people money, but they gave it to those that are in need. Now these false prophets took the people money, home, and land, and they didn't give the money out to the poor people that were in need. But these false prophets took the peoples' money, house, and land for themselves. The Bible says that they went from house to house breaking bread. The Bible did not say that they live in the community. This is how these false prophets deceive many, and they are false preachers. They take the people money in tides and offering, and buy homes, land, and cars, and they talk about look what the Lord has blessed me with. Because they have these houses, land, cars, and nice clothing, but they were suppose to take that money to give to the poor people and the poor saints. But they didn't do that; they took the money for themselves. They are not following the apostles' doctrine. The apostles give the money out to the people, but they didn't keep anything for themselves. Now you see what the false prophets do with those communities. They take all the people money and their possessions, and leave them with nothing.

Acts 4:34-35

"Neither was there any among them that lacked: for as many as were possessors of lands or houses sold them, and brought the prices of the things that were sold." Now they sold their lands and houses to give to the poor that was in need. Verse 35

"And laid them down at the apostles feet: and distribution was made unto every man according as he had need." Now you see the apostle give out the money to the poor saints that was in need. Now what prophet or preacher nowadays take the money that people gives them, and gives it out to the poor people. But now they take the money for themselves, and they call themselves Christians. They make merchandise out of you by selling books and radio, then they ask you for an offer of $80.00.1 will give you the radio because when you are given the radio it is supposed to be free. Then when you put your price on the radio for $80.00 as an offering, you are really selling it. They try to deceive the people because you don't want to pay your tax to the government. But you better pay your taxes to the government, and stop trying to deceived the people. Then when somebody confronts you with it, you want to get all bent out of shape and mad; just like a mad dog. Just because you don't want to pay your taxes, you try to make the person say that $80.00 is an offering, But the truth is that the person is buying the radio, and then the first thing a false prophet will say is why you are listening to me? Christ didn't ask the Pharisee why do you listen to me? Paul didn't ask the Jews why do you listen to me? He wants the Jews to listen to him because when you preach the gospel, you want the people to listen to you. Like I said, the apostles did not live in the community, but they traveled. They met at the church, and they went from house to house breaking bread. I haven't found anywhere, where the Bible says that they live in a community. All are doctrine of men. The prophets and preachers supposed to pick up an offering from the people to help the poor people, especially the saints. But not for themselves to buy cars, houses, land, but for radio time on the air; these false prophets and preachers want the people to support them for radio time on the air. That money supposed to be picked up for the poor saints. The apostle picks up the money and gives it out to the poor people, but not for radio time on the air or for themselves. It's okay to take some for airtime and for yourself because you have to send out tapes and letters, but most of that money suppose to go to the poor saints. These false prophets and preachers take the people's money, and they never give money out to the poor saints. Why do people support these men? I don't know, but I guess it's because they are deceived. They can't see because they don't search the Bible. People don't support these men that don't tell you the truth, and don't give money out to the poor saints. May God give you wisdom to understand his word. Now read Acts 2:45-46 and Acts 4:34-37. Now you can see which one of us is telling the truth. Now support the preachers, and teachers that tell you the truth, and that give money to the poor saints. Thank you, may God bless his people. In Acts 2:38, the prophet from South Carolina says that isn't anywhere in the Bible where it says what name to be baptized in. Well he can't see that because he is deceived, and he was talking about how you don't have to say anything when you baptize someone, but that is not true. He says the name of the authority but it is not found anywhere in the Bible where it says to be baptized in the name of authority. Now he just wants to deny the name of the Lord Jesus Christ. He is a deceiver ladies and gentlemen, the Bible clearly tell you what name to be baptized in. This is why the Lord Jesus Christ says there shall be many false prophets, if it were possible they shall deceive the very elect. But the elect will know God's words; so that, they won't get deceived by these false prophets. Now I will read Acts 2:38, "Then Peter said unto them, Repent, and be baptized every one of you in the name of Jesus Christ, for the remission of sins, and ye shall receive the gift of the Holy Ghost." Now the Bible clearly tells you what name to be baptized in. If you can't understand that, you have been deceived. These false prophets will deceive many. They are arrogant, and they don't want to admit that they are wrong.

Now turn to Luke 24:47

"And that repentance and remission of sins should be preached in his name among all nations, beginning at Jerusalem." Now you see that the Bible says that repentance and remission of sins should be preached in his name. It does not say in the authority, it says in his name, and that the Lord Jesus Christ. Now you people rather believe man than the word of God.

John 14:26

"But the comforter, which is the Holy Ghost, whom the Father will send in my name, he shall teach you all things, and bring all things to your remembrance, whatsoever I have said unto you." You see the Lord wants you to do all things in his name. The Holy Ghost will come in his name.

1 Corinthians 1:12-13

"Now this I say, that every one of you saith, I am of Paul; and I of Apollos; and I of Cephas; and I of Christ." Now Paul was saying that some people were saying that I am of Paul, Apollos, Cephas and Christ. So Christ is not divided. Verse 13

"Is Christ divided? was Paul crucified for you? Or were ye baptized in the name of Paul?" Now Paul asked if he were crucified for them. No he was not, Christ was crucified for us. Then Paul asked if ye were baptized in the name of Paul? Now Paul was letting them know that the name that they were baptized in were in the name of Jesus Christ. Now one false prophet said that you don't have to say anything to baptize someone. Oh how the false prophet deceive the people. Now I ask the people, why do you keep giving your money to people that tell lies to you? If you try to correct the prophets and preachers, they refuse correction. If they refuse correction, then separate yourself from these people and don't support those men because they are deceiving other people. The people go after these men in the community. You see what the Lord said in Luke 21:8, "And he said, Take heed that ye be not deceived: for many shall come in my name, saying, I am Christ; and the time draweth near: go ye not therefore after them." Many people run to those communities where the false prophets are, and they deceive many. Some of these false prophets say that it will be a hundred and forty-four thousand of all the tribes of the children of Israel plus the multitude of the Gentiles. The one from South Carolina says that.

In Revelation 7:9, the false preachers, teachers and prophets talk about a great multitude, which no man could number, is of all the Gentiles' nations. They are grafted into the tribes of the children of Israel.

Read Romans chapter 11, it will tell you. Then where it says a great multitude, which no man could number, these false prophets say that means that the beast system could not number them or put their mark on them. That is true, but that is not what it is, saying in that verse to be patient with me. I will explain what the Bible is saying in that verse so be patient with me. Now most people do not want to accept that the hundred and forty-four thousand were sealed and that is all that will be saved until the beginning of the world until Christ come back.

In Revelation 7:4, John says "And I heard the number of them which were sealed: and there were sealed and hundred and forty and four thousand of all the tribes of the children of Israel." John says he "heard the number of them which were sealed: He did not see the people. He just heard the number of them, which were sealed. Then in verse 9 he said, "After this I beheld." Beheld means to see, to gaze upon, and to look at. Now you see in verse 9 John says, "After this I beheld, and lo, a great multitude, which no man could number, of all nations, and kindreds, and people, and tongues, and that include Israel to all nations stood before the throne, and before the lamb, clothed with white robes, and palms in their hands;" So just like when you walk into the Super Dome, you hear the man announce on the speaker that there are ninety thousand and one hundred twenty-one people in here. Now then you look at the people that would be a great multitude of people to you. You could not number how many people were in that Super Dome just by looking at them. Only the computer would know by how many tickets were sold, and how many people came in with their ticket. So by you just looking at the people you could not say how many people were in that Super Dome. You see when John looks at the people before the throne in verse 9. They were from all nations, and that was the same hundred and forty-four thousand of all the tribes of the children of Israel, because the Gentiles are grafted into the tribes of the children of Israel. That is all that will be saved because the saints were chosen before the foundation of the world, and God know how much people he will save. Now I want to go back to explain a little bit more of what I left out in Revelation 14:1-3,

Revelation 14:1

"And I looked, and lo, a lamb stood on the mount Zion, and with him a hundred forty and four thousand, having his Father's name written in their foreheads." You see the Lord stood on the mount Zion with just a hundred and four thousand. Verse 2

65

"And I heard a voice from heaven, as the voice of many waters, and as the voice of a great thunder: and I heard the voice of harpers harping with their harps:" The voice of many waters is the Lord Jesus Christ. Verse 3

"And they sung as it were a new song before the throne, and before the four beasts, and the elders: and no man could learn that song but the hundred and forty and four thousand, which were redeemed from the earth." The elders that are in heaven is probably the one's that God created first in heaven. We called them elders here on earth and where it says, "no man could learn that song but the hundred and forty and four thousand, which were redeemed from the earth." There was other people there that were in the flesh that went into the millennium, and they had to come worship the Lord."

Turn to Zechariah 14:16

"And it shall come to pass, that everyone that is left of all the nations which came against Jerusalem, shall even go up from year to year to worship the King, the LORD of hosts, and to keep the feast of tabernacles." Now you see this is why just the hundred forty and four thousand could learn that song, the one that was saved. So the people that were left of all the nations could not learn that song, but only the hundred forty and four thousand could learn that song. Verse 4

"These are they which were not defiled with women; for they are virgins. These are they which follow the lamb whithersoever he goeth. These were redeemed from among men, being the first-fruits unto God and to the lamb." So you have to divide the word of truth. Now it says this, "These are they which were not defiled with women; for they are virgins." Now some people think that these people never had sex with women, but that is not so if you divide the word of truth.

2 Corinthians 11:2

"For I am jealous over you with godly jealousy: for I have espoused you to one husband, that I may present you as a chaste virgin to Christ." You see a chaste virgin means that you become a new creature in Christ, and you won't be indulging in unlawful sexual activity. Just like a new car, they call it a virgin because its never been used like a young lady that never had sex. So when you are born again, you become a new creature, a virgin.

2 Corinthians 5:17

"Therefore, if any man be in Christ, he is a new creature: old things are passed away; behold, all things are become new." Now the next dividing in the word of truth is where it says, "which follow the lamb whithersoever he goeth."

Revelation 3:4

"Thou hast a few names even in Sardis which have not defiled their garments; and they shall walk with me in white: for they are worthy." You see they are virgins; they are not defiled.

Revelation 17:14

"These shall make war with the lamb, and the lamb shall overcome them; for he is Lord of lords, and king of kings; and they that are with him are called, and chosen, and faithful." That is the saints that are with him; the Jews and the Gentiles.

Revelation 7:15

"Therefore are they before the throne of God, and serve him day and night in his temple: and he that sitteth on the throne shall dwell among them." Now these are all the saints from all nations before the throne of God.

Revelation 7:17

"For the lamb which is in the midst of the throne shall feed them, and shall lead them unto living fountains of waters: and God shall wipe away all tears from their eyes." So these are all the saints, the Lord will have one fold. "And God shall wipe away all tears from their eyes." Thank God amen

Back to Revelation 14:4 where it says, "were redeemed from among men," for more detail turn to Revelation 5:9, "And they sung a new song, saying, Thou art worthy to take the Book, and to open the seals thereof: for thou wast slain, and hast redeemed us to God by thy blood out of every kindred, and tongue, and people, and nation;" So now you see the Bible tells you where they came from that were before the throne of God. You see they came from, "out of every kindred, and tongue, and people, and nation;" The Bible explains itself in different parts of the Bible. "The hundred forty and four thousand, having his Father's name written in their foreheads." These are all the saints from all nations including the nation of Israel that stood before the throne, and before the lamb clothed with white robes and palms in their hands; Now I hope everyone understand what I have explained. May God bless you all and give you all the wisdom to understand his word about the hundred forty and four thousand.

Back to Revelation 14:4 where it says, "being the first-fruits unto God and to the lamb." And then it goes to James 1:18, "Of his own will begat he us with the word of truth, that we should be a kind of first-fruits of his creatures." The saints are the firs-fruits of his creatures, and he begat us with the word of truth. The first resurrection is the first-fruits. May God bless you all with the wisdom, and support the preacher or the teacher that tell you the truth that they may help the other poor saints like the apostles did in Act 2:45 and Act 4:34-37. You can read this on your own. Now I will talk about another error of the prophets, teacher and the seven thunders. The seven thunders are the seven angels, which had the seven trumpets. Now you see the seven thunders are the seven angels. Oh the errors of the prophets and I heard one of the prophets and the teachers say that the first thunder was when George Bush and Golucheurf met on the High Sea of the Mediterranean that was the first thunder, but that is not true. The second is when the pope came to Denver, Colorado, but that is not true. The third one is when the wise men, the religious people came to Chicago, and he said that was the third thunder, but that is not true. So that prophet said the thunders were sealed up. Yes it was sealed up, but later on the Lord told John to seal not the sayings of the prophecy of this Book. So the thunders are not sealed up to them that understand.

Revelation 10:3

"And cried with a loud voice, as when a lion roareth: and when he had cried, seven thunders uttered their voices." Now rightly dividing the word of truth where it says, "seven thunders uttered their voices."

Revelation 8:5

"And the angel took the censer, and filled it with fire of the altar, and cast it into the earth: and there were voices, and thunderings, and lightnings, and an earthquake." You see the voices are the seven angels that had the seven trumpets. Verse 6

"And the seven angels which had seven trumpets prepared themselves to sound." The seven thunders are the seven angels, but right now we are in the first trumpet: hail and fire mingled with blood, and they were cast upon the earth. So right now, when we have stormy weather, we have hail in the land. Then when the summer and fall gets here, we have fire in the land, and the trees and grass are being burnt up. Then right now we are having violence in the land killing, war and bloodshed.

Revelation 10:4

"And when the seven thunders had uttered their voices, I was about to write: and I heard a voice from heaven saying unto me, seal up those things which the seven thunders uttered, and write them not." So he told John to seal up those things which the seven thunders uttered and write them not, but in verse 11 he told John to prophecy again. Verse 11

"And he said unto me, Thou must prophesy again before many peoples, and nations, and tongues, and kings."

Revelation 22:10

"And he saith unto me, seal not the sayings* of the prophecy of this book: for the time is at hand." The prophecy of this book is not sealed up, so the seven thunders are not sealed up. So the seven thunders are the seven angels that had the seven trumpets. When you here thundering and lightning, that means something is coming and something is going to happen. That's why the seven angels prepared themselves to sound. Just like now, when you have thundering and lightning, that mean most likely the rain is coming. Many of these false prophets say that we are in the fourth or fifth trumpet, but that is not true. Saying that we been hearing of war since World War I and World War II, but Jesus Christ was talking about the end time right now starting from 9/11. Now we are just starting to see wars and rumor of wars, but the end is not yet, and these false prophets claiming that the end is here now. But Jesus Christ said, "And ye shall hear of wars, and rumours of wars: see that ye be not troubled: for all these things must come to pass, but the end is not yet." These false prophets claim that the end is here now, but the Lord said there shall be many false prophets, but the mark of the beast is not out good yet, and these false prophets and preachers think that the mark of the beast will come out after the antichrist show up. The mark of the beast will come out before that antichrist set up the abomination that maketh desolate, but he will probably pass a law; that everybody must have a mark in their right hand, or in their foreheads, "And that no man might buy or sell, save he that had the mark, or the name of the beast, or the number of his name." Now everybody won't receive the mark of the beast, and some will receive the name of the beast or the number of his name. All that worships the image of the beast, and receives the mark in their right hands, or in their forehead will be cast into the lake of fire. When enough people receive the mark of the beast, then that antichrist will obligate everyone to have the mark of the beast, the name of the beast or the number of his name that no man might buy or sell. Just like the Insurance Company did for cars, when a whole lots of people voluntarily got insurance for their cars then they pass a law that it is mandatory to have insurance on your car. That the same thing that the antichrist will do when enough people get the mark of the beast, then he will make it mandatory that no man might buy or sell. Save he that had the mark, or the name of the beast, or the number of his name. That takes time; years don't just happen overnight, and these false prophets say that the end is here now. We are just in the beginning of wars and rumors of war, and evil will go forth from nation to nation just like in the first Babylon. The end is not yet because all things that are written must be fulfilled.

Oh the error of the prophet is like one of the prophets from South Carolina. He says that Jesus Christ is not the son of man now, but that is not true. He is the son of man now, and he is coming back as the son of man with power and great glory.

Now turn to Acts 7:56

"And said, Behold, I see the heavens opened, and the son of man standing on the right hand of God." You see Jesus Christ is the son of man right now in heaven. And I heard a false prophet say that Jesus Christ is not the son of man now in heaven. The one from South Carolina is that prophet, but that is not true. Jesus Christ is the son of man now in heaven, and he is coming back as the son of man. The Lord said there shall be many false prophets. Yes, Jesus is coming back as the son of man.

Turn to Matthew 26:64, and it read like this, "Jesus saith unto him, Thou hast said: nevertheless, I say unto you, Hereafter shall ye see the son of man sitting on the right hand of power, and coming in the clouds of heaven." Now he is coming back as the son of man, and people believe everything what these false prophets be telling them. They will turn against you and hate you. They just take man's word over God's word because they don't know the word of God, and He will try them as by fire. Just like when you go and try to get your driving license, the man tell you to study this book and to come back in a few days. When you come back, the man will test you and he will try you. He will give you a test, ask questions, and put false answers before you, so he will try you. He may put four answers before you, but only one of those answers is correct; so he is trying you. Only two of the answers will be very close. So you have to know that book to pick the correct answers. The same thing is for the word of God. God will put false preachers, false teachers, and false prophets before you. So if you don't know the Bible as his word, these false prophets, preachers, and teachers will deceive you. This is why God gives you the Bible as his word for you to study, so that you won't get deceived. Some of these prophets, preachers, and teachers will tell you mostly everything the truth, but they will have errors in some places in their teaching. They will refuse correction, so that makes them false prophets, preachers, and/or teachers.

71

So this is why the Lord said "if it were possible, they shall deceive the very elect." but the elect will know God's word. They will study the book, so that these men will not deceive them. They will do like the Berea did with Paul. They searched the scriptures daily, whether those things are true what these men were saying. It is like the false prophet saying that Jesus Christ is not the son of man now in heaven, and that is not true. Jesus Christ is the son of man now in heaven. People believe that lie that Jesus Christ is not the son of man now in heaven. Oh the error of those prophets, and the people cannot see that darkness is upon them. Gross darkness is upon the people, and they cannot think because they have no wisdom and no knowledge because they refuse correction; so they are in darkness. I will talk about another error of the prophets because the people follow the doctrine of men. Now that false prophet probably will claim that he did not say that, but he did say that Jesus Christ is not the son of man now in heaven. He will claim that he did not say that, and he will probably say that the people are lying on him. He is just deceiving you.

Now I want to get back to another error of the prophet like about the white horse in Revelation 6:2, and the false prophet from South Carolina and some of those other prophets say that the rider on the white horse in Revelation 6:2 is thee antichrist, but that is not true. The rider on the white horse in Revelation 6:2 is Jesus Christ. He judges, and he makes war. That is what he is doing right now, making war to destroy the wicked. The prophets are in darkness, and the one from South Carolina say that he is telling the truth, but that is not true. If you say that Jesus Christ is not the son of man now in heaven, then you are lying. He says the last forty five days is the great tribulation, but that is a lie. Just like the lie about the seven thunders, the daily sacrifice, and these other prophets too, like on end time prophecy. They believe that the daily sacrifice is an animal sacrifice now, but that is not true. I am trying to warn the people about these false prophets. This is why! wrote this book, to warn the people about the errors of the prophets, but the people are dull of hearing for the Bible says, "For the heart of this people is waxed gross, and their ears are dull of hearing, and their eyes, have they closed; lest they should see with their eyes, and hear with their ears, and understand with their heart, and should be converted, and I should heal them." That's the people right now in this generation. They will turn against you for these false prophets, but they have ears to hear you. But they cannot understand, because they are deceived and the prophets are deceived. He will say that he is not deceiving you, but I am telling you the truth. The prophets that deceive people won't tell you that they are deceiving you. The people that listen and believe that prophet won't say that that prophet is deceiving them because they are deceived by the prophet. This is why the people will turn against you for these false prophets because they don't know that they are deceived by them because they don't know the word of God. But I want to talk about Revelation 6:2, about the rider on the white horse that is Jesus Christ. Now I will rightly divide the word of truth.

Revelation 6:2

"And I saw, and behold, a white horse: and he that sat on him had a bow; and a crown was given unto him: and he went forth conquering, and to conquer." Now some of these preachers, teachers, and prophets say this rider is not the same rider as in Revelation 19:11-12 because these false prophets, teachers, and preachers say this rider in Revelation 6:2 had a bow with no arrow. But the truth is God uses a bow and arrow, the bow and arrow goes together. I am sorry that I have to repeat myself, but I want to make sure people understand.

Turn to Psalms 7:11-13 and it says this: "God judgeth the righteous, and God is angry with the wicked every day. If he turn not, he will whet his sword; he hath bent his bow, and made it ready."

Verse 13

"He hath also prepared for him the instruments of death; he ordaineth his arrows against the persecutors." You see God uses arrows. The bow and the arrow go together. Now the people believe these false prophets, preachers, and teachers over the word of God because they can't think. They don't have any wisdom and knowledge of God's word, and when you correct them, they refuse correction. These false prophets and preachers know that you are right, but they will say that you are wrong because they refuse correction. They don't want anyone to tell them anything because they are drunk and mad in this Babylonian system. They have drunk the wine of her fornication, so they are mad.

There are two types of people that you cannot tell them anything: a drunk person and a mad person.

Now in Revelation 6:2, these false prophets and preachers say that the rider had one crown, which is the antichrist, but that is not true. That is Jesus Christ on that white horse in Revelation 6:2, but I will tell you a little more about the bow later.

Turn to Lamentation 2:4

"He hath bent his bow like an enemy: he stood with his right hand as an adversary and slew all that were pleasant to the eye in the tabernacle of the daughter of Zion: he poured out his fury like fire." God uses his bow on Jerusalem in the first Babylon. These false prophets say that God doesn't use a bow, but they are liars. Now back to the one crown. These false prophets say that rider only had one crown, so that is the antichrist, but that is not true. It is Jesus Christ.

Now turn to Revelation 14:14

"And I looked, and behold, a white cloud, and upon the cloud one sat like unto the son of man, having on his head a golden crown, and in his hand a sharp sickle." The Lord had on his head a golden crown. He had one golden crown on his head, and these false prophets said that is the antichrist in Revelation 6:2. That is false because in the fifth trumpet that is when that antichrist showed up because the first seal, the first trumpet, and the first vail all starts and all end at the same period of time. All the way to the seventh, they all end at the same period of time.

Daniel 7:4

"The first was like a lion, and had eagle's wings;" Verse 5

"a second, like to a bear," Verse 6

"After this, I beheld, and lo, another, like a leopard," That was the third beast.

Now in verse 7 is the fourth beast. How can you say that was the antichrist when the first seal open up? The first beast is first. The lion and the eagle's wings is Britain and the United States. These are whom you are watching now in Iraq. We are in the first seal and in the first trumpet. That antichrist showed up in the fifth trumpet. You have to think, and put the pieces together. The Bible is like a puzzle, you have to put the pieces together by what comes first; ask God for wisdom and listen to people. Check everything out by the word of God. Now rightly dividing the word of truth in Revelation 6:2 where it says, "a white horse:" Let's go to Zechariah 6:3 and Revelation 19:11.

Zechariah 6:3

"And in the third chariot white horses; and in the fourth chariot grizzled and bay horses." The horses are the spirits of the heaven, and these false prophets are talking about how that is the antichrist. On that white horse is the British empire. The Bible clearly tells you that the horses are the spirits of the heavens. Now you see what it says in Zechariah 6:4, "Then I answered and said unto the angel that talked with me, What are these, my Lord?" Verse 5

"And the angel answered and said unto me, These are the four spirits of the heavens, which go forth from standing before the Lord of all the earth." They are the four horses in Revelation chapter 6. The horses are the spirits of the heavens, and these men are talking about that the antichrist are the British empire. God send these spirits so that the nation may fight one another. So the Lord judges and makes war, and that is what he is doing now. When he open up the first seal, it is to judge and make war.

Now back to Revelation 19:11

"And I saw heaven opened, and behold, a white horse; and he that sat upon him was called faithful and true, and in righteousness he doth judge and make war." When the twin towers came down on 9/11, that was when the seal was opened. When the seal is opened, he starts to judge and make war. In Revelation chapter 19 is the same white horse as in chapter 6 of Revelation. Now back to Revelation 6:2, "And he that sat on him had a bow;" it goes to Psalms 45:4,5. Now you will see who is on the white horse. Now verse 4

"And in thy majesty ride prosperously because of truth and meekness and righteousness; and thy right hand shall teach thee terrible things." That is the Lord that is riding on that horse. Now verse 5

"Thine arrows are sharp in the heart of the king's enemies; whereby the people fall under thee." You see the Lord's arrows are sharp in the heart of the king's enemies. When he opens the seal, he is starting to destroy the wicked people. This is why we are having wars and rumors of war. But the end is not yet because we are only in the first beast. The lion with eagle wings and that is Britain and the United States that we are watching now.

Back to Revelation 6:2 where it says, "and a crown was given unto him:" and he went forth conquering, and to conquer." For more detail turn to Zechariah 6:11 and Revelation 14:14.

Zechariah 6:11

"Then take silver and gold: and make crowns, and set them upon the head of Joshua the son of Josedech, the high priest;" Now Jesus is the high priest. Where it says to take silver and gold to make crowns, that crown is a lot of little crowns that make up the whole big crown. is the same thing you read about in Revelation 19:11, and chapter 14. In chapter 6, the Bible tells you a crown. In chapter 19, the Bible have many crowns. The many crowns make up the whole big crown. The Bible says whoso readeth, let him understand. The people don't he any understanding. They cannot think because they have no wisdom and no knowledge of God's word. They have been polluted of these false prophets and teachers. The people are so deceived; it is mind troubling because they give heed to seducing spirits: doctrine of devils. They think that by giving these false prophets and preachers thousands of dollars that they might get into heaven. If you are deceived, and stay deceived, you will not enter into God's kingdom. Jesus says to take heed and let no man deceive you. These false prophets use their tongue to deceive. They are like politics; they steal God's words from their neighbor. Like for instance he say that the United States is Babylon, and next thing he will say Roman is Babylon. So if the Vatican becomes Babylon, he will say that he told you that. Now if the United States become Babylon, he will say that I told you that. I am talking about the false prophets, even the one from South Carolina. He use his tongue to deceive the people for money. These false prophets raise up false teachers. Now in 2 Timothy 4:3, I am trying to warn you people of these false prophets so take heed.

2 Timothy 4:3

"For the time will come, when they will not endure sound doctrine; but after their own lusts shall they heap to thesdes teachers, having itching ears." For the time has come that they will not endure sound doctrine. It is here now, but they will heap to themselves teachers having itching ears like the Baptist church people. They have their own teachers, and a false prophet started it. They cannot teach in a Catholic church because they believe different from each other. Catholic cannot come teach in a Baptist church or in a Jehovah witness or kingdom hall. A Jehovah witness teacher cannot come teach in a Muslim church and it goes on and on. A false prophet started each one of those churches. Even the over comer ministry were started by a false prophet. They heap to themselves because they all believe different from one another. Paul said that he teaches everywhere in every church. This is why Paul said that they heap to themselves teachers having itching ears because each church organization has their own little teachers that were started by a false prophet. Oh the lies of the prophets, and I heard one of them say that he is the last prophet before Jesus Christ comes back, but that is not true. He said that he never said he is the last prophet, but he did say that. He is a liar. The two witnesses are the last two prophets that God will send before he comes back. God's presence will be with them, just as he was with Moses and Elijah. This prophet from South Carolina says that the two witnesses will testify and witness of him that the messenger has come. Now isn't that something, and the people believe that lie. The two witnesses will come and testify of Jesus Christ because all men testimony suppose to be of Jesus Christ, and to worship him.

Read Revelation 12:17

"And the dragon was wroth with the woman, and went to make war with the remnant of her seed, which keep the commandments of God, and have the testimony of Jesus Christ." The saints' testimony is of Jesus Christ and not of men. This prophet from South Carolina is talking about how the two witnesses will testify of him that the messenger has come. Isn't that something, and many people believe that lie because they don't know the word of God. Their ears are dull of hearing. Like I said before, they can't think because they have no wisdom, knowledge or understanding. Now you read and you show them, and you explain to them about these false prophets. They still cannot understand. They have eyes, but they cannot see. They have ears, but they cannot hear because their ears are dull of hearing.

Zephaniah 3:4

"Her prophets are light and treacherous persons: her priests have polluted the sanctuary, they have done violence to the law." This is dealing with the end time. You see the prophets nowadays are light and treacherous persons; that means untrustworthy. Now I want to talk about another error of the prophets. Now prophets suppose to speak by two or three. Even Jesus sent the men out by two.

Turn to Luke 10:1

"After these things, the Lord appointed other seventy also, and sent them two and two before his face into every city, and place, whither he himself would come." You see the Lord sent them out by two.

Turn to 1. Corinthians 14:29

"Let the prophets speak two or three, and let the other judge." Now this is the word of the Lord in the New Testament. The prophets suppose to speak by two or three. Now in the Old Testament the prophets spoke by one, but not under the new covenant. The prophets suppose to speak by two or three in the new covenant. Otherwise, if he speaks by one, he is disobeying God. Now this is what is happening to the prophets nowadays; they want to speak by one, and they are disobeying God when they prophesy. This prophet from South Carolina says that God says. "I will send my messenger." But that was under the old covenant because John the Baptist came under the old covenant. In the Old Testament, the prophet used to speak by one, but God said in the New Testament, "Let the prophets speak two or three, and let the other judge." This is why we have so many false prophets because they don't have any understanding of God's word. Oh the error of the prophets. The Lord will send two prophets before he comes back under the new covenant. He will send the two witnesses before his coming. They are the witnesses before his coming. These false prophets deceive the people by their lies because they are deceived and they deceive others. The people are blind, and they cannot see. There are so many errors of the prophets. Now I will talk about another error of the prophets and preachers.

Acts 2:39

"For the promise is unto you, and to your children and to all that are afar off, even as many as the Lord our God shall call." Now you see, the Bible say, "For the promise is unto you, and to your children and to all that are afar off," This prophet from South Carolina says when the Bible says, "to all that are afar off," he says that means that the one that is not yet born; the one that is in the future. The children that are not yet born, he says that is what that means, but that is not true. He is teaching heresy. Now I will tell you what the Bible is talking about when it says, "to all that are afar off," The Bible is talking about the Gentiles. They were afar off without Christ being aliens from the commonwealth of Israel. Now it rightly divides the word of truth in Acts 2:39 where it says, "to all that are afar off, even as many as the Lord our God shall call." For more information turn to: Acts 10:45 Acts 11:15,18 Acts 15:3,8,14 Ephesians 2:13.17

Now Acts 10:45

"And they of the circumcision which believed, were astonished, as many as came with Peter, because that on the Gentiles also was poured out the gift of the Holy Ghost." The Bible is talking about the one that were afar off are the Gentiles. Acts 11:15

"And as I began to speak, the Holy Ghost fell on them, as on us at the beginning." That is the Gentiles whom the Holy Ghost fell on them.

Acts 11:18

"When they heard these things, they held their peace, and glorified God, saying, Then hath God also to the Gentiles granted repentance unto life." The Bible is talking about the Gentiles, God granted them repentance.

Acts 14:27

"And when they were come, and had gathered the church together, they rehearsed all that God had done with them, and how he had opened the door of faith unto the Gentiles." God opened the door of faith unto the Gentiles to them that were afar off. Now, I will go to Ephesians 2:13,17. It will show you more clearly that it is talking about the Gentiles. In Ephesians 2:13 you will see who is right, the prophet from South Carolina or the word of God.

Ephesians 2:13

"But now, in Christ Jesus, ye, who sometimes were far off, are made nigh by the blood of Christ." The ones that were far off are the Gentiles.

Ephesians 2:17

"And came and preached peace to you which were afar off, and to them that were nigh." You see them that wee afar off are the Gentiles. Them that were nigh are the circumcision, the natural branch of Israel. This prophet from South Carolina says them that were afar off are those that are not yet born into the future, and that is not true. Them that were afar off are the Gentiles. Oh the error of the prophets and preachers. Now another error of the prophets, preachers and teachers are in Matthew 24:32. Some of these men say that when Israel became a nation in 1948 that was the budding of the fig tree. That is not what the Lord Jesus is saying in verse 32. Verse 32

"Now learn a parable of the fig tree; when his branch is yet tender, and putteth forth leaves, ye know that summer is nigh:" What Jesus is saying is that when you see all those things that he talked about like, "For many shall come in my name, saying I am Christ; and shall deceive many." And like wars, and rumours of wars, and many false prophets and because iniquity shall abound, the love of many shall wax cold. And like famine, earthquake, and when ye, therefore, shall see the abomination of desolation, spoken of by Daniel the prophet, stand in the holy place (whoso readeth, let him understand) and that is when that antichrist, shall set up that image in the holy place, that false prophet then shall be great tribulation. This is what Jesus Christ is talking about in verse 32. When you shall see all these things, then you know that it is near. Jesus Christ is soon to come back because he said it. Now learn a parable of the fig tree because when you see the fig tree bud, you know that summer is near. The fig tree always is the first trees to bud, and then all the other trees follow. I was raised on a farm in the country, and I know that the fig tree always is the first one to put on leaves. This is what the Lord is talking about, not when Israel became a nation. He is talking about when you see all these things are happening, and then you know that his coming is near. Oh the error of the prophet. Verse 33

"So likewise ye, when ye shall see all these things,know that it is near, even at the doors." You see when you see all these things happening; you know Christ coming is near. Now another error of the prophets is in Revelation 18:2, "And he cried mightily with a strong voice, saying, Babylon the great is fallen, is fallen, and is become the habitation of devils and the hold of every foul spirit, and a cage of every unclean and bureful bird." These prophets say that this Babylon right now has become the habitation of devils, the hold of every foul spirit, and a cage of every unclean and hateful bird, but that is not true. It becomes that after it has fallen, nor before it has fallen. That is when the great tribulation is over. becomes the habitation of devils, the bold of every foul spirit, and cage of every unclean and hateful bird. Unfortunately, these prophets can see that saying that the United States is Babylon in Revelation chapter 18, but that is not true.

To Isaiah 34:11

"But the cormorant and the bittern shall possess it; the owl also and the raven shall dwell in it: and he shall stretch out upon it the line of confusion, and the stones of emptiness." This is after Babylon has fallen and is destroyed. The birds and the owl will dwell there. Not now, but after it is destroyed. The prophets cannot even think because they are foolish. They are drunk with the wine of her fornication and are mad.

Hora 9:7

"The days of visitation are come, the days of recompense are come; Israel shall know it: the prophet is a fool, the spiritual man is mad, for the multitude of thine iniquity, and the great hatred." The spiritual man is mad. The prophets nowadays are mad also. The prophets have a great deal of hatred. This is what we are seeing now because of their iniquity; the prophets have great deal of hatred. The people that believe these prophets and follow these prophets they have a great hatred too. They make believe that they are loving and kind, but the minute you try to tell them and show them the word of God, they will not want to hear or listen to you. They won't even let you show them what the Bible says. They don't want you to show them anything. They think that you don't know the word of God, and that you don't know what you are talking about just because you are not a prophet. But God revealed things to babes; this is what the people refused to see. So they stay deceived and keep believing a lie because God sends them a strong delusion.

Remember what Jesus said in Matthew 11:25

"At that time Jesus answered and said, I thank thee, O Father, Lord of heaven and earth, because thou hast hid these things from the wise and prudent, and hast revealed them unto babes." So the people don't want anyone to tell them anything or to show them what the word of God says. They only want the false prophets or preachers to teach them the word of God. God revealed things unto babes, so the people stay deceived because they refuse correction. They cannot think. They don't have any wisdom, knowledge, or understanding,

Hosea 9:7

"the spiritual man is mad, for the multitude of thine iniquity, and the great hatred" It then goes to Ezekiel 13:3, and it continues to Micah 2:11 and Zephaniah 3:4.

Now Ezekiel 13:3

"Thus saith the LORD GOD; wo unto the foolish prophets, that follow their own spirit and have seen nothing!" These false prophets say that the Lord had told them this 5 years ago or 25 years ago, but the truth is that the Lord haven't told them anything because the Lord haven't spoken. He will speak when the two witnesses come, then he will speak to the whole world. Now he is speaking through his word in the Bible. He will confirm the covenant with the two witnesses. His presence will be with them, like he was with Moses and Aaron. Verse 6

"They have seen vanity and lying divination, saying, The LORD saith: and the LORD hath not sent them: And they have made others to hope that they would confirm the word." The LORD has not sent these lying false prophets. They just after the people's money, and they will tell you that they are not. They are liars, and the truth is not in them. Verse 7

"Have ye not seen a vain vision, and have ye not spoken a lying divination, whereas ye say. The LORD saith it, Albeit I have not spoken?" The Lord has not spoken to these false prophets and preachers. They claim that the Lord has told them this and that, but the Lord hasn't spoken.

Micah 2:11

"If a man walking in the spirit and falsehood do lie, saying, I will prophesy unto thee of wine and of strong drink; he shall even be the prophet of this

83

people." Now these are the kind of prophets the people like nowadays; they like false prophets.

Zephaniah3:4

"Her prophets are light and treacherous persons: her priests have polluted the sanctuary, they have done violence to the law." Her prophets are light that means they can be seen and they are untrustworthy. They take the people tithes and offering, and they don't give the poor people anything. They commit adultery, and they deceive the people by their lies. They teach false doctrine, and they steal God's word from their neighbor and every one of these prophets. They are untrustworthy, and they just want the people's money.

Now another error of the prophets is in Luke 17:34, "I tell you, in that might there shall be two men in one bed; the one shall be taken, and the other shall be left." These false prophets say the one that is taken is the wicked one, but that is not true. The one that is taken is the righteous one, but these false prophets say otherwise. The one that is taken is the righteous, and the Bible is talking about taken up in the air to meet the Lord in the clouds on his way back down to Earth to Jerusalem. In Luke 17:34 when it say, "the other shall be left"; the other that shall be left is the wicked one.

Matthew 24:40

"Then shall two be in the field; the one shall be taken, and the other left." Verse 41

"Two women shall be grinding at the mill; the one shall be taken, and the other left." The one that is taken is the righteous, and the one that is left is the wicked.

I Thessalonians 4:17

"Then we which are alive and remain shall be caught up together with them in the clouds, to meet the Lord in the air: and so shall we ever be with the Lord." This is what the Bible is talking about: one is taken and the other is left. The one that is taken is to meet the Lord in the air, and one that is left will be destroyed. Remember what the Bible says is 2 Thessalonians chapter 1. The Lord Jesus shall be revealed from heaven with his mighty angels in flaming fire taking vengeance on the one that is left, the wicked. The one that is taken will be with him, the saints, when he comes back taking vengeance.

Psalms 91:8

"Only with thine eyes shall thou behold and see the reward of the wicked." Now you see that the saints will be with the Lord, when he destroy the wicked, the one that was left." These false prophets lie to you, and these false preachers stop believing every word these men tell you, and study God's word for yourself. God bless you all. The two witnesses are coming soon so be patient. God bless.

Daniel 9:24

"Seventy weeks are determined upon thy people and upon thy holy city, to finish the transgression, and to make and end of sins, and to make reconciliation for iniquity, and to bring in everlasting righteousness, and to seal up the vision and prophecy, and to anoint the most Holy." Now verse 24 to 27 is talking about Jesus Christ, and some of these false prophets, preachers, and teachers claim that verse 27 is talking about the antichrist, but that is not true. Now rightly dividing the word of truth in Daniel 9:24 where it says, "and to make reconciliation for iniquity", which means making peace between enemies because we were enemies of God. We were sinners, and where it says, "to make reconciliation for iniquity" turn to Isaiah 53:10 for more insight.

Isaiah 53:10

"Yet it pleased the LORD to bruise him; he hath put him to grief: when thou shalt make his soul an offering for sin, he shall see his seed, he shall prolong his days, and the pleasure of the Lord shall prosper in his hand." So Jesus Christ was an offering for our sins, and making union of Jews and Gentiles.

Now turn to Romans 5:10

"For if when we were enemies, we were reconciled to God by the death of his son; much more, being reconciled, we shall be saved by his life." Now back to Daniel 9:24 where it says, "and to bring in everlasting righteousness and to seal up the vision and prophecy," Jesus Christ brought in everlasting righteousness. For more details turn to: Isaiah 53:11 Jeremiah 23:5,6 Hebrews 9:12 Revelation 14:6

Now you see if you read those verses on your own that I gave you, then you will see that Jesus brought in everlasting righteousness by the shedding of his own blood for many. Now the next dividing is where it says, "and to anoint the most Holy." That is Jesus Christ. For more information turn to: Palms 45:7 Luke 1:35

John 1:41 Hebrews 9:11

You can read these verses on your own as well. You see Christ came as our High priest. He is the anointed one. Now if you read those verses that I gave to you, you will see that Jesus Christ is the High Priest, the anointed one. In Daniel 9:25 I will explain this verse because most people do not understand this verse, but be patient. I will explain it to you if it is the will of the Lord, but first I will read the verse to you. "Know therefore and understand, that from the going forth of the commandment to restore and to build Jerusalem unto the Messiah the prince shall be seven weeks, and threescore and two weeks: the street shall be built again, and the wall, even in troublous times." First of all this prophecy is being explained by one day, is one year.

Turn to Numbers 14:34

"After the number of the days in which ye searched the land, even forty days (each day for a year shall) ye bear your iniquities, even forty years; and ye shall know my breach of promise." Breach means a violation of a law so the children of Israel murmured against God.

Ezekiel 4:6

"And when thou hast accomplished them, lie again on thy right side, and thou shalt bear the iniquity of the house of Judah forty days: I have appointed thee each day for a year." Each day stands for a year. Now back to Daniel 9.25, "from the going forth of the commandment to restore and to build Jerusalem unto the Messiah the Prince," Jerusalem was destroyed in the first Babylon by Nebuchadnezzar. God sent Nebuchadnezzar against Jerusalem because the people had sinned against God, and they had not repented for their sins. So God sent Nebuchadnezzar against Jerusalem to destroy it. Now after Babylon, the commandment was to restore and build Jerusalem again, until Jesus came the first time. Now you can read about the restoration of Jerusalem in Ezra chapters 4, 6 and 7, and in Daniel 9:25 Now it says, "shall be seven weeks, and threescore and two weeks:" Now seven weeks is 49 days, so the will be forty nine years. Now the seven weeks are for the building of the temple in Jerusalem.

Now turn to John 2:19-20. "Jesus answered and said unto them destroy this temple, and in three days I will raise it up." Now verse 20, "Then said the Jews, forty and six years was this temple in building, and wilt thou rear it up in three days." Now you see this temple was forty and six years. This was the temple in building. That was the seven weeks the temple was being built. Now one week is seven years. Two weeks is fourteen years. Three weeks is twenty one years. Four weeks is twenty eight years. Five weeks is thirty five years. Six weeks is forty two years. Seven weeks is forty nine years.

So the temple building was complete in the seven weeks, which was forty six years. Now I hope you understand what I have explained to you. The seven weeks were the building of the temple, but it got completed in forty six years. So that was in the seven weeks. Now some of these false prophets, preachers, and teachers are talking about when Israel became a nation in 1948, and the 49 years started from that point until 1997; that makes forty nine years. They say that Jesus Christ was going to come back thee and a half years after that so that will be in 2000 he was going to come back. Some said by 1997. Now we find out that they are liars, even the prophet from South Carolina said that Jesus Christ was going to come back by the year 2000 or before the year 2000. He said there was no doubt in his mind, and this prophet from South Carolina just flat out lied to the people. He says that he didn't say that, and a man played his tape on the radio where he did say that. Jesus Christ was going to come back by the year 2000, or before the year 2000. He said there was no doubt in his mind. This man is just a flat out liar, and this is why he doesn't play all of his old tapes on the air because everyone would catch him in his many lies. Plus if he does play some of them, he try to erase part of the tape so the people won't catch him out of his lies. Now let me move on, but I am just trying to show God's people how these prophets, preachers and teachers deceive the people by their smooth talk and by their fair speech. Now back to Daniel 9:25 where it says, "and threescore and two weeks. That is sixty-two weeks. The sixty- two weeks are from the time that the temple was completed until Jesus Christ came and died on the cross. Now 62 weeks is 434 years, plus the seven weeks make forty nine years for the completion of the temple, which adds to equal 483 years. So from the time the commandment went forth to restore and build Jerusalem, until the time that Jesus Christ died on the cross made 483 years. Verse 26

"And after threescore and two weeks shall Messiah be cut off, but not for himself: and the people of the prince that shall come shall destroy the city and the sanctuary, and the end thereof shall be with a flood, and unto the end of the war desolations are determined." Now rightly dividing the word of truth where it says, "shall Messiah be cut off," for more information turn to: Isaiah 53:8 Mark 9:12 Luke 24:26,46

Isiah 53:8

"He was taken from prison and from judgment: and who shall declare his generation? For he was cut off out of the land of the living: for the transgression of my people was he stricken." You see after the completion of the temple, and after the 62 weeks, Messiah was cut off for the transgression of his people.

Mark 9:12

"And he answered and told them, Elias verily cometh first, and restoreth all things; and how it is written of the Son of man, that he must suffer many things, and be set at nought." So that means he was going to be cut off. Luke 24:26

"Ought not Christ to have suffered these things, and to enter into his glory?" That means that he was going to be cut off. Verse 46

"And said unto them, Thus it is written, and thus it behooved Christ to suffer, and to rise from the dead the third day." That means that Christ was to suffer and be cut off. Now the next dividing of the word truth is in Daniel 9:26 where it says, "the people of the prince that shall come." That is the Lord's army that he sent against Jerusalem in 70 A.D. to destroy the city and sanctuary just like he did in the first Babylon. He sent Nebuchadnezzar the king of Babylon to destroy Jerusalem in the first Babylon because the people had gotten wicked. They persecuted the saints and kill some, and this is what they are starting to do now: persecute the Christians. Now the same thing will happen to Jerusalem again at this end time. God will send the antichrist his army against Jerusalem to destroy the city and the sanctuary, but that will happen when they kill the two witnesses. Then Jerusalem will be taken over by the Gentiles, and then they will set up the abomination that maketh desolate. That is an image that they will set up like Nebuchadnezza did. Now where it says, "the people of the prince that shall come" it the goes to:

Matthew 22:7

"But when the king heard thereof, he was wroth: and he sent forth his armies, and destroyed those murderers, and burned up their city." Now you see that was the Lord Jesus Christ that sent forth his army to destroy those murderers and bum up their city because the so-called Christians always persecute the real Christians. They even kill some like they did Stephen. They stoned him; the so-called Christians are the ones that know a little about the word of God, and they persecute the real Christians. They believe what they been taught, but it was a false doctrine. They persecute the real Christians like they did Jesus and Paul. So this is why God always sent fort his army to destroy those murderers. The same thing will happen at the end time, even with the two witnesses. Now the next dividing in the word of truth is where it says, "shall destroy the city." Let's turn to: Luke 19:44

"And shall lay thee even with the ground, and thy children within thee; and they shall not leave in thee one stone upon another: because thou knowest not the time of thy visitation." You see Jerusalem will be made desolate because of their sins, and they don't want to repent. So the Lord will send the antichrist and army against Jerusalem. The next dividing is where it says, "and the sanctuary;" It then goes to Matthew 24:2

"And Jesus said unto them, See ye not all these things? Verily I say unto you, there shall not be left here one stone upon another, that shall not be thrown down." Now you see most of these preachers and prophets say that happened in 70 A.D. when the temple was destroyed, but that will happen again in the last days, Jerusalem shall go forth into captivity in the last days for three and a half years. Now the next dividing is in verse 26 where it says, "and the end thereof shall be."

For more insight turn to Matthew 24:6

"And ye shall hear of wars, and rumours of wars: see that ye be not trouble: for all these things must come to pass, but the end is not yet."

Now this is where we are right now, at the beginning of wars and rumors of wars. The Lord says the end is not yet. Verse 14

"And this gospel of the kingdom shall be preached in all the world, for a witness unto all nations; and then shall the end come." You see the gospel of the kingdom have to be preached unto all nations, and then shall the end come. The gospel of Christ is all the same gospel from Genesis to Revelation. The next dividing of the word of truth is where it says, "With a flood, and unto the end of the war desolations are determined." For more information turn to: Isaiah 8:7,8 Daniel 11:10,22 Nahum 1:8

Isaiah 8:7

"Now therefore, behold, the Lord bringeth up upon them the waters of the rivers, strong and many, even the king of Assyria, and all his glory: and he shall come up over all his channels, and go over all his banks:" That means that he will have a mighty strong army. Verse 8

"And he shall pass through Judah; he shall overflow and go over, he shall reach even to the neck; and the stretching out of his wings shall fill the breadth of thy land, O Immanuel." And that will repeat itself in the last days because we have sinned against our God

Daniel 11:10

"But his sons shall be stirred up, and shall assemble a multitude of great forces: and one shall certainly come, and overflow, and pass through: then shall he return, and be stirred up, even to his fortress." So that army will be a great multitude, an overflowing army. Verse 22

"And with the arms of a flood shall they be overflown from before him, and shall be broken; yea, also the prince of the covenant." "yea, also the prince of the covenant" and some of these false prophets say that is the antichrist, but that is not true. The prince of the covenant is Jesus Christ. He made a covenant with his people. The antichrist will come against Jesus Christ's people. So Jesus Christ is the prince of the covenant. Now rightly dividing the word of truth where it says, "yea also the prince of the covenant."

Daniel 8:10

"And it waxed great, even to the host of heaven; and it cast down some of the host and of the stars to the ground, and stamped upon them." You see the Bible says, "even to the host of heaven, he waxed great" against Christ, the prince of the covenant. Verse 11

"Yea, he magnified himself even to the prince of the host, and by him the daily sacrifice was taken away, and the place of his sanctuary was cast down." Now you see where it says, "even to the prince of the host", the prince of the host is Jesus Christ. By the antichrist, the daily sacrifice was taken away. That means he killed the two witnesses and some of the saints, and put some in prison. He was taking away the daily sacrifice because the daily sacrifice is not an animal sacrifice

91

in the new covenant in the New Testament. I pray that God will help you all understand his word.

Daniel 8:25

"And through his policy also be shall cause craft to prosper in his hand; and he shall magnify himself in his heart, and by peace shall destroy many: he shall also stand up against the prince of princes; but he shall be broken without hand." Now you see he shall also stand up against the prince. Jesus Christ is the prince, and the prince of peace.

Nahum 1:8

"But with an overrunning flood he will make an utter end of the place thereof, and darkness shall pursue his enemies." That means it will be a great army and desolations will be determined. You see there shall be a great earthquake, famine, pestilence and wars. This is all starting right now. It is just the beginning of it, the beginning of sorrow. Thank God that his word is being fulfilled, and those that are seeking God better get right with God before it is too late. I thank everyone for listening and God bless you all.

I am going to talk about speaking in tongues. Now many people do not understand what speaking in tongues is. They think that speaking in tongues means that you do not know what you are saying, but that is so true. The apostles knew what they were saying when the day of Pentecost fully came. Now remember in Genesis 11:1 where it says that the whole world was of one language and the people were trying to build a tower up to heaven. God came down to confound their language so that they may not understand one another's speech. Now on the day of Peste, God gives the apostles to speak those languages that he cofounded in Genesis. Then the word of truth is rightly divided in 4 where it says, "they were all filled with the Holy Ghost".

Acts 1:5

"For John truly baptized with water; but ye shall be baptized with the Holy Ghost not many days hence." So the disciples were baptized with the

Holy Ghost, but some of the preachers believe that there are 2 baptisms, but there is only one baptism. When the Bible talking about the baptism with the word "S" on it, he is talking about the baptism of John. The other baptism is that of the Lord Jesus Christ, which is the Holy Ghost. So if you use John's baptism, you won't receive the gift of the Holy Ghost. So there is only one baptism, and that is in the name of Jesus Christ. I will talk about it later. Now back to Acts 2:4 where it says, "to speak with other tongues, as the spirit gave them utterance", let's get more insight and turn to: Mark 16:17 Acts 10:46 Acts 19:6 1 Corinthians 13:1 1 Corinthians 14:2

Mark 16:17

"And these signs shall follow them that believe: In my name shall they cast out devils; they shall speak with new tongues;" Now you have to read God's word very carefully, and slowly look at all of God's words that are talking about speaking in tongues. Study and meditate day and night on his word. So it says that they shall speak with new tongues; it is talking about the body of Christ. The body of Christ has many members, some apostles, prophets, teachers, and some speak with tongues and some interpret. Not everyone spoke in tongues. The Bible explains itself in different parts of the Bible. The Bible is like a puzzle; the parts are not usually all in one place. His words are not usually found all in one verse of the Bible. Knowledge has vanished from the preachers. One believes this, and the other believes that. Neither one has the truth; they all speak lies. They don't want anybody to tell them nothing or explain anything to them. They harden their heart and stiffen their neck like the false prophets in Jeremiah's time; they refuse correction.

Acts 10:46

"For they heard them speak with tongues, and magnify God. Then answered Peter," So they heard them speak with tongues because God wanted them to speak with tongues in other languages. If God didn't want you to speak in other languages, you will not speak in other languages. Speaking in tongues is a gift from God. The apostles didn't have to go to school to learn these languages. He gave them those languages in that moment when the Holy Ghost came down, so they could go and teach the gospel into all nations and to every creature.

Jesus told his disciple in Matthew 28:19

"Go ye therefore and teach all nations, baptizing them in the name of the Father, and of the Son, and of the Holy Ghost;" Now you tell me how the disciple was going to teach all nations if they could only speak but one language, which is Galilean. So God gives them the gift to speak all these languages so they can go and spread his word to all nations. This is what he told them in Matthew 28:19. Remember God's word was only given to the Israelite people in the Old Testament. The word was not given to the Gentile nations in the Old Testament, and the Gentile nations would speak a lot of different languages. Now remember in Genesis 11:1 where it says, "And the whole earth was of one language, and of one speech." Look up the meaning of the word "tongues". It will tell you that it means the primary organ used for speech and tasting, a language. Now you see the whole earth was of one language. The people were trying to build a city and a tower up to heaven.

Genesis 11:5-7

"And the LORD came down to see the city and the tower, which the children of men builded. And the Lord said, Behold, the people is one, and they have all one language; and this they begin to do: and now nothing will be restrained from them, which they have imagined to do. Go to, let us go down, and there confound their language, that they may not understand one another's speech." Now you see tongues is a language. God confound the people's language, which is why we have different languages in the world today. On the day of Pentecost, God filled the apostles with the Holy Ghost. God gives them all the language and tongues that are here on earth, so that they can go and teach all nations. And a lot of these preachers and church people claim that they are speaking in tongues, but they are just murmuring something with their mouth. It is a so called made up language. They don't know what they are saying themselves. The apostles knew what they were saying. They were speaking in the other people's language, telling them about Jesus in their language. The apostles could speak these other people's language. Theses church people hear these preachers over the radio claiming that they speak with tongues when they can't speak but only one language. Speaking in tongues is speaking in different languages like French, Japanese, Spanish, German and so forth. God didn't give then the gift of speaking in tongues. So now they want to fake it, and they are claiming that they are following the apostles doctrine, but they are not. The apostles spoke in those other people's language. That is what the Bible call speaking in tongues. Well some of them say that you don't understand me because I am speaking in an unknown tongue, but he or she don't know what they are saying themselves, like when a man come from Japan. He came into a church house and started speaking Japanese, and everybody in that church could only speak English. So that means that he would be speaking with an unknown tongue to the church people because nobody in that church speaks Japanese. That man was supposed to translate his speech, meaning he should speak English so that the people could understand him. The Bible does say that they suppose to speak by two or three in 1 Corinthians 14 27-28

"If any man speak in an unknown tongue, let it be by two, or at the most by three, and that by course; and let one interpret. But if there be no interpreter, let him keep silence in the church; and let him speak to himself, and to God." Now these false preachers and prophets are talking about when you speak in an unknown tongue, nobody knows what you are saying, according to 1 Corinthians 14:27, Someone knows what the man is saying that speak his language. The Bible says, "If any man speak in an unknown tongue, let it be by two, or at the most by three, and that by course; and let one interpret." You see somebody knows what the man is saying that speak his language. Some of these preachers so-call filled with the Holy Ghost says what it means to be filled with the Holy Ghost. This is the evident of speaking in tongues that they have to speak a made up language. This is the doctrine of men. They add and take away from God's words. Some of them say when you speak in an unknown tongue, you are speaking in a heavenly language, but the Bible did not say that. This is the doctrine of men. The apostle spoke in those people's language here on Earth. God gives these apostles power to raise people from the dead. Now you think that God couldn't give the apostles power to speak in other languages like French, Japanese, Spanish, German, and so forth. He gives them power to raise people from the dead. God has all power. He gives the language to the birds and animals. When the birds and animal speak to each other, God understands what they are saying to each other, the same way like when a man comes into a church house speaking Japanese but everybody in the church house only speaks English. So nobody knows what the man is saying, but God knows what he is saying because he gave him that language. So to the people in the church house that only speak English, the man is speaking with an unknown tongue. Most people will not understand even though I explain it to them. They will not understand because they harden their heart. They don't want anybody to show them anything or to tell them anything. But "God shall send them strong delusion, that they should believe a lie: because they love not the truth." I have so much to say to the people about a lot of false doctrine that are being taught by these false preachers and teachers in the church. They claim that they are filled with the Holy Ghost, but they are not. Mostly every preacher in each church claim that they are filled with the Holy Ghost and so-called speaking one language, and that is English. They deceive the people with lies claiming that they are following the apostle's doctrine. The apostle spoke in those other people's language.

Acts 19:6

"And when Paul had laid his hands upon them, the Holy Ghost came on them; and they spake with tongues, and prophesied." Now you see when these men read that verse in the Bible, they say you see whe Paul laid his hands upon them, the Holy Ghost came on them; and they spake with tongues, and prophesied. They forgot about all the rest of the verses, about speaking in tongues. These men spoke in tongues because God wanted them to speak in tongue. We don't have any say so what we want. God gives us what he wants us to have. Now we can ask God for the best gifts. If that's his will for us to have it, he will give it to us. The Bible explains itself in different verses in the Bible like what is says in 1 Corinthians 14:27-28. I will explain it again so that the people might understand. "If any man speak in an unknown tongue, let it be by two, or at the most by three, and that by course; and let one interpret." The Bible didn't say that man that spoke in an unknown tongue is not a Christian, but they supposed to let them speak by two or at the most by three and that by courses and let one interpret. Now you see all people do not speak with tongues. Verse 28

"But if there be no interpreter, let him keep silence in the church;" Now the Bible says that man suppose to keep silence in the church because he cannot speak those people's language. So the Bible says, "and let him speak to himself, and to God" because God knows what the man is saying in his language, but the people in the church do not understand him; therefore, he suppose to have an interpreter

1 Corinthians 12:10

"To another, the working of miracles; to another, prophecy; to another, discerning of spirits; to another, divers kinds of tongues; to another, the interpretation of tongues:" So why these men always talking about the gift of speaking in tongue like that's the only gift God gives to the people. God gives the gift of prophecy, the working of miracles, and many other gifts. You don't hear about these preachers talking about these gifts, and they preach about the same thing every week like they don't know anything else in the Bible. They suppose to teach from Genesis to Revelation, but they don't do that. They still on milk, and they try to tell somebody about speaking in tongue. They don't even know what speaking in tongue is. These false preachers try to say that speaking in tongue is a heavenly language, but that is not what the Bible says. Speaking in tongues is like speaking in other people's language here on Earth because the apostles spoke those people's language. The Bible explains itself in different parts of the Bible. All did not speak in tongue at that time. The Bible says, "knowing this first, that no prophecy of the scripture is of any private interpretation." Some people look at one scripture, and use their own interpretation. They ignore the rest of the scripture that is talking about the same thing. So they get deceived, and deceive other by their lies. When someone tries to correct them, they refuse correction because they are deceived. They say that they are not, but they are.

1 Corinthians 12:28

"And God hath set some in the church, first apostles, secondarily prophets, thirdly teachers, after that miracles, then gifts of healings, helps, governments, diversities of tongues." Most of you still cannot see this. God has some apostles, not all; some prophets, not all; miracles, not all; some gifts of healings, not all; some helps, not all; some governments, not all; some diversities of tongues, not all. Now all do not have these gifts. Some may have all, some one or two. Now you will look at Mark 16:17. You cannot answer it, unless you lie about it; try to explain it with your lies. You see the Bible explains itself in different parts of the Bible.

1 Corinthians 12:29

"Are all apostles? Are all prophets? Are all teachers? Are all workers of mirades?" No. Verse 30

"Have all the gifts of healing? Do all speak with tongues? Do all interpret?" No. Now you see Paul asks a question, "do all speak with tongues?" The answer is no, and these false preachers get on the radio and claim that everybody spoke in tongues at that time. If that was the case, everybody at that time was apostles, preachers, teachers and miracles. Then everybody was a gift of healings, helps, and government. Now you know that everybody does not work in government office positions and everybody was not speaking diversity of tongues. Paul is letting you know that everybody did not speak in tongues just like everybody were not apostles, prophets, teachers and so forth. You see knowledge has vanished from the preachers, teachers and prophets. They don't have any understanding of God's word. Paul asked, "do all interpret?" No all do not interpret.

1 Corinthians 13:8

"Charity never faileth: but whether there be prophecies, they shall fail; whether there be tongues, they shall cease; whether there be knowledge, it shall vanish away." The Bible says that charity never fails. Charity is love.

The Bible also says, "whether there be prophecies, they shall fail:" Prophecies are failing now just like Jesus Christ said in Matthew 24:5,11,24. Many false prophets shall arise, and this is where we are now: false teaching and false prophecy. The Bible says "whether there be tongues, they shall cease;" So tongues have ceased from the people because nowadays, all of a sudden you don't see people speaking in other people's languages without going to school to learn these languages. The apostles did not have to go to school to learn those other people's language. God filled the apostles with the Holy Ghost, and they spoke in those other people's language immediately, in that moment, when the Holy Ghost came down. Now these church people are faking speaking in tongues, but they are not; they are liars, and they are deceiving people. The Bible says whether there be knowledge, it shall vanish away. You see knowledge has vanished from the preachers and the people because the people are wicked; they reject knowledge. They don't want anyone to correct them, so they reject knowledge, and knowledge has vanished away. I heard one preacher say that knowledge has not vanished, but that is not true. Knowledge has vanished from the people. I heard a teacher over the radio say that all the gifts have ceased, but the Bible did not say that. It says, "whether there be tongues, they shall cease;" The Bible did not say that all the gifts shall cease; it says tongues shall cease, not the rest of the gifts. This is how we spread false doctrine, by not reading God's word very carefully. It says knowledge shall vanish away. God say his "people are destroyed for lack of knowledge:"

Hosea 4:1

"Hear the word of the LORD, ye children of Israel: for the LORD hath a controversy with the inhabitants of the land, because there is no truth, nor mercy, nor knowledge of God in the land." This is where we are right now, no knowledge of God in the land. The truth has perished from their mouth like when I heard that teacher on the radio saying how all gifts have ceased. If all the gifts have ceased, why is he still on the radio teaching? Teaching is a gift from God because if it were not from God, you would teach falsely. Verse 6

99

"My people are destroyed for lack of knowledge: because thou hast rejected knowledge, I will also reject thee, that thou shalt be no priest to me: seeing thou hast forgotten the law of thy God, I will also forget thy children." They will tell you, "Ye are not under the law, but under grace?" That is true, but I will explain this at another time if it is the will of the Lord. I have so much to tell you about a lot of false teaching that the preachers are teaching you. This is why God's people are being "destroyed for lack of knowledge: because thou hast rejected knowledge," God is starting to punish the people right now, but they cannot see, they are blind. The blind are leading the blind, and they both shall fall into the ditch. The people are supporting these blind leaders with their tithes and offering, giving their money to them to spread more false doctrine. The Bible did not say that you have to pay tithes in the New Testament. The Bible says, give; not grudgingly, for God loveth a cheerful giver. So these preachers lie to you and say that you suppose to give ten percent of your earnings. The Bible did not say that in the New Testament. They deceive most of these men and especially the women because they don't know the scripture. So don't give these preachers your money to help them spread lies.

The Bible says in 2 Corinthians 9:7, "Every man according as he purposeth in his heart, so let him give; not grudgingly, or of necessity: for God loveth a cheerful giver." So the Bible did not say that you have to give your tithes in the New Testament, but you can read Acts 2:45 and Act 4:34-35. But if it will be the will of the Lord, I will explain all of this at another time. But don't let these preachers deceive you by taking your money and telling you lies. I don't support any man that tells me lies because he only will spread more lies. So you need to check everything what these men are telling you by the word of God, so that you won't get deceived.

1 Corinthians 13:1

"Though I speak with the tongues of men and of angels, and have not charity, I am become as sounding brass, or a tinkling cymbal." Paul can speak different languages of men and of angels because God gave him the gift of speaking in tongues. Remember God gives the animal different languages from the people, and the angels can speak different languages from the people here on Earth because God has made man a little lower than the angels.

1 Corinthians 14:2

"For he that speaketh in an unknown tongue, speaketh not unto men, but unto God: for no man understandeth him; howbeit in the spirit he speaketh mysteries." So he that speaks in an unknown tongue, speaks not unto men because the people who he is speaking to do not speak his language. So he is speaking mysteries to them like if that man can only speak German, and we can only speak English, so that man is speaking mysteriously to us. But that man is speaking to God because God knows what that man is saying because God gave him that language. He gives all the language here on Earth. So this is why Paul said that "him that speaketh in an unknown tongue, pray that he may interpret." That means to speak the other person's language. That is the same thing you read about in verses 27 and 28. You see in the New Testament, Jesus Christ sent the people out by two. Jesus sent his disciples out by two and in Luke 10:1 you can read that. This is why these preachers cannot explain 1 Corinthians chapter 14 because they don't know what it means to speak in tongue and in an unknown tongue. They make believe that they are explaining it, but when you ask them about this part in the Bible, they ignore it because they cannot even answer. If they do answer, they will answer it wrong. They got the wrong understanding about speaking in tongue, and speaking in an unknown tongue. Verse 3

"But he that prophesieth, speaketh unto men to edification, and exhortation, and comfort." So he that prophesized is speaking the people's language that he is speaking to. Upon one's faith to instruct to building the church, and to encourage others to commendable conduct. Verse 4

"He that speaketh in an unknown tongue edifieth himself; but he that prophesieth edifieth the church." So "He that speaketh in an unknown tongue edifieth himself;" because he understand what he is saying in his language. So he is instructing himself because nobody there understands him because he is speaking in an unknown tongue. Verse 5

"I would that ye all spake with tongues, but rather that ye prophesied: for greater is he that prophesieth than he that speaketh with tongues, except he interpret, that the church may receive edifying." Now Paul said, "I would that ye all spake with tongues," Now you see Paul is letting you know that everyone did not speak in tongues. Now if you cannot understand that everybody did not speak in tongues because God has blinded your eyes, and these preachers believe that everyone that gets baptized suppose to speak in tongue. Or everyone that is saved, suppose to speak in tongues. They cannot even speak in tongues themselves. They try to fake it with a language they made up themself, but they are blind; they cannot see.

Now you read what the Bible says in John 12:39-40

"Therefore they could not believe, because that Esaiahs said again, He hath blinded their eyes, and hardened their heart; that they should not see with their eyes, nor understand with their heart, and be converted, and I should heal them." This is what is happening to the people right now. They are blinded by these false preachers and teachers, "Speaking lies in hypocrisy, having their conscience seared with a hot iron;" Now back to Acts 2:5, "And there were dwelling at Jerusalem Jews, devout men, out of every nation under heaven." That means that they were religious men out of every nation under heaven. Verse 6

"Now when this was noised abroad, the multitude came together, and were confounded, because that every man heard them speak in his own language." So the people were confused because every man from all nations and all languages heard the apostles speak to them in his own language. Now you see the apostles were speaking to those people in their own language out of every nation, and many nations were speaking different languages like they are now. So speaking in tongues is speaking in different languages that are here on Earth now. Verse 7

"And they were all amazed, and marveled, saying one to another, Behold, are not all these which speak, Galileans?" Now you see, the apostles could only speak Galileans before they were filled with the Holy Ghost. Now when the Holy Ghost came, they could speak all the languages that were in the world, so they could teach all nations. Verse 8

"And how hear we every man in our own tongue, wherein we were born?" These men heard the apostles speak in their language where they were born. Speaking in tongue is speaking in other people's language, so you can communicate with each other. If someone cannot speak your language, you cannot communicate with that person. Verse 9

"Parthians, and Medes, and Elamites, and the dwellers in Mesopotamia, and in Judea, and Cappadocia, in Pontus, and Asia," Verse 10

"Phrygia, and Pamphylia, in Egypt, and in the parts of Libya about Cyrene, and strangers of Rome, Jews and proselytes," Verse 11

"Cretes and Arabians, we do hear them speak in our tongues the wonderful works of God." The apostles spoke all those nations language that I just read. Now this is what speaking in tongues is, speaking in other people's language. God had sent them a strong delusion, that they should believe a lie because they believe not the truth. Now if you read 2 Thessalonians chapter 2, I will start in verse 9. I am going to talk about Bible prophecy Matthew chapter 24. Verse 3

"And as he sat upon the mount of Olives, the disciples came unto him privately, saying, tell us, when shall these things be? And what shall be the sign of thy coming, and of the end of the world?" The disciples ask Jesus a question, "What shall be the sign of thy coming, and of the end of the world?" So Jesus Christ told his disciples all the signs, and what will be happening at that time. Now some of these false preachers, teachers, and prophets say that we won't be here during that time, during the great tribulation. But I will show you that the saints will be here during the great tribulation, and some of these false preachers, teachers and prophets say that Jesus Christ came back in 70 A.D. Matthew chapter 24 already happened in 70 A.D. so if that's true, where is Jesus Christ? The Bible says the saints shall rule and reign with him.

Now turn to 2 Timothy 2:12 and it reads like this, "If we suffer, we shall also reign with him: if we deny him, he also will deny us:" So why are we not reigning with him in Jerusalem? Where is he? Well I will tell you. He won't come back until all things are fulfilled, and then he is coming back.

103

But in Thessalonians 2:9, "Even him, whose coming is after the working of Satan, with all power, and signs, and lying wonders", this is what we are having now: signs and lying wonders.

Now in Daniel 7:18

"But the saints of the most High shall take the kingdom, and possess the kingdom for ever, even for ever and ever." The saints will be ruling right here on Earth with Christ in this physical and spiritual kingdom when Christ comes back and set up a kingdom. You can read about it in Daniel 2:44. Now back to Matthew 24:3 where it divides to say, "tell us, when shall these things be? And what shall be the sign of thy coming, and of the end of the world?" So Jesus Christ answered them, and he told them all what is going to be happening at the end of the world. The disciples knew that they weren't going to be living when that time comes. Jesus is talking to the saints that will be living when that time comes, and that time has arrived. We are in the first trumpet, but there are many people that don't know that. Now back to Matthew 24:4, but will talk about the seal and the trumpets another time.

Matthew 24:4

"And Jesus answered and said unto them, Take heed that no man deceive you." It divides where it says, "take heed that no man deceive you." Let's turn to Ephesians 5:6 Colossians2:8,18

2 Thessalonians 2:3

1 John 4:1

Ephesians 5:6

"Let no man deceive you with vain words: for because of these things cometh the wrath of God upon the children of disobedience." Now you see God says, "let no man deceive you" because the wrath of God cometh upon the children of disobedience, so that when you let a man deceive you, the wrath of God comes upon you. So take heed and check out everything that these preachers be telling you about the word of God.

Colossians 2:8

"Beware lest any man spoil you through philosophy and vain deceit, after the tradition of men, after the rudiments of the world, and not after Christ." The church people are not following after Christ. They are following after the tradition of men like when they are so-called speaking in tongue. Christ is coming "immediately after the tribulation" like these prophets be talking about the willing wall. They say that will come down, but the Bible is talking about the wall that Israel is putting up right now around the Palestinean area and Jerusalem. The Lord will throw the wall down with a stormy wind and an overflowing shower with great hailstones and even probably the willing wall will be throw down somehow. You can read about it in Ezekiel 13:10-15. These false prophets spoke out of their own heart. Verse 18

"Let no man beguile you of your reward in a voluntary humility and worshipping of angels, intruding into those things which he hath not seen, vainly puffed up by his fleshly mind," This is what we see now in these false prophets "vainly puffed up by his fleshly mind". They don't want any man to correct them, so they are deceived and deceive others.

2 Thessalonians 2:3

"Let no man deceive you by any means: for that day shall not come, except there come a falling away first, and that man of sin be revealed, the son of perdition;" Now the falling is already here. The man of sin will be revealed the son of perdition, because the people are wicked, and preachers are teaching falsely. All of them speak lies, and they refuse correction. They preach only for money, to get these fine homes and nice cars. They deceive these men and especially women for their money.

1 John 4:1

"Beloved, believe not every spirit, but try the spirits whether they are of God; because many false prophets are gone out into the world." Now what are that time. There are many false prophets, and the people love to have it this way.

Mathew 24:5

"For many shall come in my name, saying, I am Christ; and shall deceive many." It divides where it says, "For many shall come in my name, saying, I am Christ;" then for more detail turn to:

Jeremiah 14:14

Jeremiah 23:24-25

Mathew 24:24

John 5:43

Jeremiah 14:14

"Then the LORD said unto me, The prophets prophesy lies in my name: I sent them not, neither have I commanded them, neither spake unto them: they prophesy unto you a false vision and divination, and a thing of nought, and the deceit of their heart." So they will come in Jesus Christ name saying that He is Lord. He is Christ. But their prophecy is false, and their teaching is false. They are not coming in the name of the Lord.

Jeremiah 23:24

"Can any hide himself in secret places that I shall not see him? Saith the LORD. Do not I fill heaven and earth? Saith the LORD." You see nobody can hide himself from the Lord because the Lord has heard what the prophets said. They prophesy lies in his name. Verse 25

"I have heard what the prophets said, that prophesy lies in my name, saying, I have dreamed, I have dreamed." This is what the prophets are saying in this day in time. They speak from their own heart. They steal the Lord's "words every one from his neighbour." They steal it from the internet or from people calling in on the radio or from books. You see they are not getting the word directly from the Lord. They use their tongues and say that the Lord told them this, but the Lord has not spoken to them. Yet they tell their lies.

Matthew 24:24

"For there shall arise false Christ, and false prophets, and shall shew great signs and wonders; insomuch that, if it were possible, they shall deceive the very elect." This is what we are seeing right now, false Christs and false prophets. There are many of them. Just about every one of them is false. Now back to Matthew 24:5 where it says, "and shall deceive many." Then it goes to verse 11, "many false prophets shall rise, and shall deceive many." Many shall be deceived because people always want to be where the big crowd is. They think that it is where the truth is being preached because of the crowd of people. This is why they have a crowd of people there, and most people love crowds. The people like it there, but they don't tell you about your sins. They teach you false things because these false Christs and false prophets are deceived. A deceiver won't tell you he is deceiving you because he is deceived. The people that he deceives won't admit that they are deceived by the deceiver because they are deceived by the deceiver. You cannot tell anything or show anything in the Bible to a deceived person. They don't want to listen because they are deceived by the deceiver. Now let's read John 5:43.

John 5:43

"I am come in my Father's name, and ye receive me not: if another shall come in his own name, him ye will receive." It's just like when these preachers, teachers, and prophets be saying that when the Jews go back to sacrificing bulls and goats, animal sacrifices, that will be the abomination that maketh desolate, but that is not true. These men come into their own name and the people will believe them or they will be rapture out of the earth before the great tribulation, but that is not true. The preachers, teachers, and false prophets come in their own name because they are deceived and they deceive others.

God said in Job 12:16

"With him is strength and wisdom: the deceived and the deceiver are his." If that person be deceived, God deceived that person. You can read about it in 2 Thessalonians 2:10-12.

Matthew 24:6

"And ye shall hear of wars, and rumours of wars: see that ye be not troubled: for all these things must come to pass, but the end is not yet." Now you see now we have wars, and that is just the beginning. When 9/11 hit, President Bush said it will be war, and this is what we are having now. The first seal was opened up on 9/11, and then then trumpet when we went to war with Iraq. We have hail and fire mangled with blood in the land and around the world. You don't see when we have stormy weather in the land. We have hail when we have stormy weather. In the summer and fall, we have fire in the land. A third part of the trees and grass burn in the United States, especially in the western states and in other countries like Australia and other places in the world. We have bloodshed in the land in other parts of the world. We have war and violence in the land and around the world. They were eating, drinking, marrying and given in marriage. That is what the people are doing now, eating. This is why American people are over weight, and other countries too. They are eating too much. They are fulfilling Bible prophecy, and drinking too much. Marrying and divorcing leads to violence because they give women rights over men because men have gotten wicked. Man don't want to obey God anymore, and the women don't want to obey him either. The children don't want to obey neither one of them. So the world is filed with violence. The first seal is opened up, and the first trumpet has sounded. Some of these men said that the seal has been opened up since World War I, and some says since World War II. The Bible is talking about the end time when the seal is opened and the trumpet sounds and the vial is poured out. All of this is at the end time. These men have been deceived by prophesying lies unto you, and now they are all confused. God is bringing judgment on the people because we have sinned against God, and we have not kept his commandments. We have left all of God's commandments because of the false prophets, teachers, and peachers. There are many of them. This is why God is bringing terror on us. This is why we have terrorism.

Leviticus 26:14-16

"But if ye will not hearken unto me, and will not do all these commandments; And if ye shall despise my statutes, or if your soul abhor my judgments, so that ye will not do all my commandments, but that ye break my covenant: I also will do this unto you, I will even appoint over you terror, consumption, and the burning ague, that shall consume the eyes, and cause sorrow of heart: and ye shall sow your seed in vain; for your enemies shall eat it." Now you see the Lord said, "I will even appoint over you terror." This is why we are having terrorism now because we don't want to obey the Lord. Now the worst is yet to come.

Matthew 24:7

"For nation shall rise against nation, and kingdom against kingdom: and there shall be famines, and pestilences, and earthquakes in divers places." Now I will show you in the scripture this is the Lord's doing, making the nation rise against nation, and kingdom against kingdom. Men do not want to obey the word of the Lord. They don't want to stop sinning. If you divide the word of truth and turn to: 2 Chronicles 15:6 Isaiah 19:2 Haggai 2:22 Zechariah 14:13

2 Chronicles 15:6

"And nation was destroyed of nation, and city of city: for God did vex them with all adversity." That's the Lord's doing when nation rise against nation and kingdom against kingdom

This is what God is saying in Isaiah 19:2

"And I will set the Egyptians against the Egyptians: and they shall fight every one against his brother, and every one against his neighbour; city against city, and kingdom against kingdom." Why are we having war, pestilence, famine and earthquakes? Because we have sinned against God, and the people do not want to repent. God is bringing on the judgment and the worst is yet to come.

Haggai 2:22

"And I will overthrow the throne of kingdoms, and I will destroy the strength of the kingdoms of the heathen; and I will overthrow the heathen; and I will overthrow the chariots, and those that ride in them; and the horses and their riders shall come down, every one by the sword of his brother." This is why Iraq kingdom is overthrown.

Zechariah 14:13

"And it shall come to pass in that day, that a great tumult from the LORD shall be among them; and they shall lay hold every one on the hand of his neighbour, and his hand shall rise up against the hand of his neighbour." Nations will rise up against each other to fight, that is the Lord's doing. This is the Battle of Armageddon.

Matthew 24:8

"And these are the beginning of sorrows." Right now we are almost in the beginning of sorrows. Verse 9

"Then shall they deliver you up to be afflicted, and shall kill you: and ye shall be hated of all nations for my name's sake." Now this is what's going to happen to the saints right now. The so-called Christians will cause you to be put in prison and kill like they did with Jesus Christ, Paul and other disciples because they don't understand the truth. They will persecute you. Now rightly dividing the word of truth in verse 9 where it says, "Then shall they deliver you up to be afflicted, and shall kill you:" For more information let's go to:

Matthew 10:17

Mark 13:9

Luke 21:12

John 15:20

John 16:2

Acts 4:23

Acts 7:59

Acts 12:1

I Peter 4:16

Revelation 2:10

I will read a few verses for you, then you can read the rest on your own.

Matthew 10:17

"But beware of men: for they will deliver you up to the councils, and they will scourge you in their synagogues." So now is the time that we have to beware because they will cause you to be put in prison and put to death.

Mark 13:9

"But take heed to yourselves: for they shall deliver you up to councils, and in the synagogues ye shall be beaten: and ye shall be brought before rulers and kings for my sake, for a testimony against them." Now you see what will happen to some of us. He is talking to the saints that will be living in the end time. This is what is starting to happen right now. Thank you Lord Jesus for your words are being fulfilled.

Luke 21:12

"But before all these they shall lay their hands on you, and persecute you, delivering you up to the synagogues, and into prisons, being brought before kings and rulers for my name's sake." Now the true church will go through persecution. Now friends and kinfolk will betray one another and cause them to be put to death.

You can read the rest of the verses on your own. I would like to go back to 1 Corinthians 14:1. I would like to start back again in 14:1-29

1 Corinthians 14:1

"Follow after charity, and desire spiritual gifts, but rather that ye may prophesy." It divides where it says, "desire spiritual gifts."

1 Corinthians 12:31

"But cover earnestly the best gifts. And yet shew 1 unto you a more excellent way." Paul is saying that you have to earnestly desire the best gifs. Now the next dividing is in verse 1 where it says, "but rather ye may prophesy." From there turn to:

Numbers 11:25-29

"And the LORD came down in a cloud, and spake unto him, and took of the spirit that was upon him, and gave it unto the seventy elders: and it came to pass, that when the spirit rested upon them, they prophesied, and did not cease." Now the Lord took the spirit of Moses and gave it unto the seventy elders. Verse 29

"And Moses said unto him, Enviest thou for my sake? would God that all the LORD's people were prophets, and that the LORD would put his spirit upon them!" Moses said that all the LORD's people were prophets, but all of God's people are not prophets. He set some in the church to be prophets, teachers and so forth. These false prophets and teachers claims that everybody that is a Christian should speak in tongue, but that is not true. Anyway tongue has ceased, but I will get to that later. Now I want to explain myself again in 1 Corinthians 14:2.

1 Corinthians 14:2

"For he that speaketh in an unknown tongue, speaketh not unto men, but unto God: for no man understandeth him; howbeit in the spirit he speaketh mysteries." Now it divides where it says, "speaketh in an unknown tongue, speaketh not unto men, but unto God:"

Acts 2:4

"And they were all filled with the Holy Ghost, and began to speak with other tongues, as the Spirit gave them utterance." Now the Bible says, "he that speaketh in an unknown tongue, speaketh not unto men, but unto God:" because God knows what that person is saying because that person is not speaking in your language, but God knows what that person is saying because he gave all of these different languages in Genesis chapter 11. The whole world were one language, and the people were trying to build a tower up to heaven, and God came down and confounded their language, so that they may not understand one another. This is why we have these different tongues, languages, around the world. God filled the apostles with the Holy Ghost, so that they might go into nations, tongues and languages to preach the gospel to all people. God gave the apostles the ability to speak all these languages that he gave to the people in Genesis chapter 11. When he confound their language, and on the day of Pentecost when he came down, he gave the apostles the Holy Ghost to speak all those languages that he gave to the people in Genesis chapter 11. The apostles could speak all these languages. He told his disciples to go and teach all nations. How they were going to teach all nations, and they could only speak Galileans. Now speaking in tongues is speaking in the other person's language. Now on the day of Pentecost, these men that were from different nations and languages hear the apostles speaking in tongues. The apostles started speaking in their language and telling them about Jesus Christ to repent for their sins. Now speaking in tongue is speaking in that other person language. Now speaking in an unknown tongue to that person, that person doesn't understand what you are saying to him because that language is unknown to him. He cannot speak that language until that person interprets it to him; that means speak his language. So now that person is speaking in tongue. The apostles could speak those other nation's languages, and this is why these people from those nations said, "that every man heard them speak in his own language." These false prophets and teachers say that the apostles did not speak in these other nation's languages. Even the one from South Carolina say that the apostles did not speak in these other nation's languages, but that is not true. The apostles did speak in those other nation's languages, and he says when a person speak in an unknown tongue, he do not know what he is saying; but that is not true. Now why did the Bible say this? "If any man speak in an unknown tongue, let it be by two or three and let one interpret, or if there be no interpreter." Why the one that interprets knows what the man is saying? "Let him keep silence in the church; and let him speak to himself, and to God." So if he is speaking to himself and to God, he knows what he is saying. Now you see how these false prophets and teachers have no understanding of the word of God.

1 Corinthians 14:3

"But he that prophesieth, speaketh unto men to edification, and exhortation, and comfort." Now he that prophesies speaks unto men because he is not speaking in an unknown tongue. He is prophesying in that person's language or to the church people. Verse 4

"He that speaketh in an unknown tongue edifieth himself; but he that prophesieth edifieth the church." Now he that speaks in an unknown tongue instructs himself because he knows what he is saying. The other people in the church do not understand him because he is speaking in an unkown tongue; therefore, he is instructing himself, "but he that prophesieth edifieth the church." means that he who prophesies, instruct the church. Verse 5

"I would that ye all spake with tongues, but rather that ye prophesied: for greater is he that prophesieth than he that speaketh with tongues, except he interpret, that the church may receive edifying." Paul says, "I would that ye all spake with tongues." All of the saints did not speak in tongues at that time. These lying false prophets and teachers claim that everybody that received the gift of the Holy Ghost must speak in tongues, but that is not true. They are lies and perverts of the truth because the Bible says, "tongues, they shall cease;" Tongues shall cease anytime in the future from the time that Paul said it.

1 Corinthians 13:8

"Charity never faileth: but whether there be prophecies, they shall fail; whether there be tongues, they shall cease; whether there be knowledge, it shall vanish away." Now "charity never faileth:" means that is love, love never fails, "but whether there be prophecies, they shall fail;" There are many false prophets and their prophecy that have failed. After they see it didn't happen the way they said it would, they try to change their prophecy. That is what makes them a false prophet. With a true prophet, things happen the way that they said it would. Speaking in tongues is a gift from God, like all of the rest of the gifts. These false prophets, teachers, and preachers do not say that everybody is filled with the Holy Ghost because they know that if the prophecy doesn't come true, everybody will know that they are false and they are not filled with the Holy Ghost. That is why they use speaking in tongues, so they can use a made up language. They call it speaking in tongues, but they don't know what they are saying themselves. They try to deceive the people that they are speaking in tongues. Paul said he would rather that the people prophesy than to speak in tongues, except he interpret.

Verse 7

"And even things without life giving sound, whether pipe or harp, except they give a distinction in the sounds, how shall it be known what is pipe or harped?" Paul is saying even things without life give sound, like music. If you play a song with music and singing or play the song with just the music, you will know what song is being played by the sound. If the sound is unknown, then you won't know what is being played. It's like speaking in an unknown tongue; you won't know what that person is saying. When a person is speaking not in your language or speaking in another language, there is a distinction in the sound that comes out. Each language has a different sound. If you do not understand the sound of that language that comes out of that person's mouth, then that person is speaking in an unknown tongue to you. Verse 8

"For if the trumpet give an uncertain sound, who shall prepare himself to the battle?" If a person is speaking to you in an unknown tongue, he is giving an uncertain sound. Then you won't know what he is saying, or what to do. Verse 9

"So likewise ye, except ye utter by the tongue words easy to be understood, how shall it be known what is spoken? For ye shall speak into the air." Paul is saying that when you speak, you would be speaking for nothing because that other person or the church do not understand that person. Verse 10

"There are, it may be, so many kinds of voices in the world, and none of them is without signification." Now Paul say, "it may be, so many kinds of voices in the world," he is talking about tongues, different languages. He says none of them are without meaning. There are so many different languages in the world. Verse 11

"Therefore, if I know not the meaning of the voice, I shall be unto him that speaketh a barbarian, and he that speaketh shall be a barbarian unto me." Paul is saying if he doesn't know the meaning of that language, which means that he doesn't understand that language. "I shall be unto him that speaketh a barbarian, and he that speaketh shall be a barbarian unto me." If someone speaketh unto you a language that you do not understand, he is a barbarian unto you, and you will be a barbarian unto him. Verse 12

"Even so ye, forasmuch as ye are zealous of spiritual gifts, seek that ye may excel to the edifying of the church." The saints suppose to be interested in spiritual gifts. That says to seek that you may be superior to the edifying of the church. Verse 13

"Wherefore, let him that speaketh in an unknown tongue, pray that he may interpret." The Bible says this, which means to speak that other person's language. Pray that he may speak that other person's language. Verse 14

"For if I pray in an unknown tongue, my spirit prayeth, but my understanding is unfruitful." Paul is saying if he prays in an unknown tongue, my spirit prays, but my understanding is unfruitful. His understanding is unfruitful because he is praying in an unknown tongue. The church does not understand him because he is praying in an unknown tongue. Verse 15

"What is it then? I will pray with the spirit, and I will pray with the understanding also: I will sing with the spirit, and I will sing with the understanding also." Paul says that he will pray with the understanding; that means he will pray and the church will understand him because he will speak their language, so that the church can understand him when he pray. Now it divides where it says, "I will sing with the spirit." Let's turn to Ephesians 5:19, and then Colossians 3:16.

Ephesians 5:19

"Speaking to yourselves in psalms, and hymns, and spiritual songs, singing and making melody in your heart to the Lord," If you are speaking to yourselves and singing, you know what you are saying because you are singing in the spirit of the Lord."

Colias 3:16

"Let the word of Christ dwell in you richly in all wisdom; teaching and admonishing one another in psalms, and hymns, and spiritual songs, singing with grace in your hearts to the Lord." Now if you sing to the Lord, even spiritual songs, you sing unto the Lord with understanding. The next dividing is in verse 15 where it says, "with the understanding also." It then goes to Psalms 47:7, "For God is the king of all the earth: sing ye praises with understanding." You suppose to sing unto the Lord with understanding and praise the Lord with understanding. Some of these prophets and teachers say that when you speak in an unknown tongue, you don't know what you are saying, but that is not true. They are liars and perverts of the truth. The person that speaks in an unknown tongue knows what he is saying because the Bible tells him so in 1 Corinthians 14:27-28. You can read these verses on your own. Verse 16

"Else, when thou shalt bless with the spirit, how shall he that occupieth the room of the unlearned say Amen at thy giving of thanks, seeing he understandeth not what thou sayest?" Paul is saying if you speak in an unknown tongue to the church or to a person, pray that you may interpret; that means to speak that other person's language. If you pray or sing, the other person or the church may understand you. When you bless with the spirit, how can that person that is unlearned say "Amen" when you give thanks to God, seeing that he do not understand what you are saying. This is why you suppose to interpret or keep silence in the church. Verse 16 divides where it says, "At thy giving of thanks." For more insight let's turn too;

1 Corinthians 11:24

"And when he had given thanks, he brake it, and said, take, eat: this is my body, which is broken for you: this do in remembrance of me." The Lord wants you to give thanks for everything. Verse 17

"For thou verily givest thanks well, but the other is not edified." The person that is praying in an unknown tongue gives thanks well, but the other is not instructed because the others cannot speak his language. Verse 18

"I thank my God, I speak with tongues more than ye all:" Paul said he thank his God that he speak with different languages more than you all: Verse 19

"Yet in the church I had rather speak five words with my understanding, that by my voice I might teach others also, than ten thousand words in an unknown tongue." Paul says in the church he would rather speak five words with my understanding; that means he would rather speak five words to the church people in their language, so that they can understand him and he can teach them, then ten thousand words in an unknown tongue that no one can understand him in the church, Verse 20

"Brethren, be not children in understanding: howbeit, in malice be ye children, but in understanding be men." Paul says you come to Christ as a little child, "be not children in understand:" but to be men in understanding. Verse 21

"In the law it is written, with men of other tongues and other lips will I speak unto this people; and yet for all that will they not hear me, saith the Lord." It divides where it says, "In the law it is", then it goes to John 10:34, "Jesus answered them, Is it not written in your law, I said, ye are gods?" It is written in the law. Jesus said, "ye are gods?" with a small g You find that in Psalms 82:6. Now the next dividing is in verse 21 where it says, "written with men of other tongues and other lips will I speak unto this people:" in Isaish 28:11. Let's read in for more details.

Isaiah 28:11

"For with stammering lips and another tongue will he speak to this people." Verse 12

"To whom he said, This is the rest wherewith ye may cause the weary to rest; and this is the refreshing yet they would not hear." Now on the day of Pentecost, the Lord gave the disciples the gift of the Holy Ghost, to speak in other tongues to his people, and some Jews did not believe. You can read on down in Acts 13:45 and in other places in Acts, yet they would not hear. Verse 22

"Wherefore tongues are for a sign, not to them that believe, but to them that believe not: but prophesying serveth not for them that believe not, but for them which believe." Tongues were for a sign to them that didn't believe, so that they might believe in the Lord Jesus Christ. Verse 23.

"If therefore the whole church be come together into one place, and all speak with tongues, and there come in those that are unlearned, or unbelievers, will they not say that ye are mad?" It divides where it says, "will they not say that ye are mad?" Let's go to Acts 2:13, "others mocking, said, These men are full of new wine." They were saying that they were drunk or mad. This is what happens when the whole church comes together into one place, and all speak with tongues. There come in those that are unlearned, and they will say that they are mad that they are speaking all different languages. Verse 24

"But if all prophesy, and there come in one that believeth not, or one unlearned, he is convinced of all, he is judged of all:" Now if all prophesy, that is speaking the same language and there come in one that don't believe or one unlearned, he is convinced of all so he will believe. Verse 25

"And thus are the secrets of his heart made manifest; and so falling down on his face, he will worship God, and report that God is in you of a truth." Now if the whole church is speaking in an unknown tongue, than he won't know what the church is saying and he won't fall down and worship God.

But with prophesying, he knows what the church is saying to him in his language. Now it divides where it says, "that God is in you of a truth." For more insight turn to Isaiah 45:14 and Zechariah 8:23.

Isaiah 45:14

Thus saith the LORD, The labor of Egypt, and merchandise of Ethiopia and of the Sabeans, men of stature, shall come over unto thee, and they shall be thine: they shall come after thee; in chains they shall come over, and they shall fall down unto thee, they shall make supplication unto thee, saying, Surely God is in thee; and there is none else, there is no God." So he will say, God is in you when the whole church come together and prophesy.

Zechariah 8:23

"Thus saith the Lord of hosts; in those days it shall come to pass, that ten men shall take hold, out of all languages of the nations, even shall take hold of the skirt of him that is a Jew, saying, we will go with you: for we have heard that God is with you." Now if you speak in an unknown tongue in the church, he won't know what you are saying, But if you prophesy, you are speaking his language; then he knows what you are saying. Verse 26

"How is it then, brethren? When ye come together, every one of you hath a palm, hath a doctrine, hath a tongue, hath a revelation, hath an interpretation. Let all things be done unto edifying." It divides where it says, "hath a doctrine, hath a tongue, hath a revelation, hath an interpretation." Let's turns to verse 6 and 1 Corinthians 12:8-10. Verse 6

"Now, brethren, if I come unto you speaking with tongues, what shall I profit you except I shall speak to you, either by revelation, or by knowledge, or by prophesying, or by doctrine?" Paul is saying by speaking in tongues, what shall it profit you? Except he speaks to you by revelation, knowledge, prophesying or doctrine so that you may understand and learn.

1 Corinthians 12:8

"For to one is given by the Spirit the word of wisdom; to another, the word of knowledge by the same Spirit;" Verse 9

"To another, faith by the same Spirit; to another, the gifts of healing by the same Spirit;" Verse 10

"To another, the working of miracles; to another, prophecy; to another, discerning of spirits; to another, divers kinds of tongues; to another, the interpretation of tongues:" You see God gives different gifts to another person, and to some he gives more than one gift according to his will. He doesn't give just because you want to speak in tongue. If he doesn't give you that gift and then you try to speak a language that you made up yourself, you don't know what you are saying and this is not from God. Tongues is a gift from God. He also gives other gifts like the word of wisdom, the word of knowledge, faith by the same spirit, the gifts of healing by the same spirit, the working of miracles, prophecy, discerning of spirits, divers kinds of tongues, and interpretation of tongues. Now all of these gifts come from God, and he gives it to his people acceding to his will.

Verse 11

"Bet all these worketh that one and the self same Spirit, dividing to every man severally as he will." He divides the gifts to every man severally as he will, but the Bible says, "But covet earnestly the best gifts."

1 Corinthians 14:27

"If any man speak in an unknown tongue, let it be by two, or at the most by three, and that by course; and let one interpret." Some of these false teachers, preachers, and prophets say that if you speak in an unknown tongue that nobody knows what you are saying, but that is not true. The person that speaks your language knows what you are saying, and God knows what you are saying. You see how that false prophet from South Carolina lies to you. The Bible clearly tells you that. "If any man speak in an unknown tongue, let it be by two, or at the most by three, and that by course; and let one interpres." That means the person that interprets knows what the person is saying, that is speaking in an unknown tongue. Now do you see how these prophets, teachers and preachers lie to you? Verse 28

"But if there be no interpreter, let him keep silence in the church; and let him speak to himself, and to God." An interpreter is a person who translates one language to another language. Now the Bible says, "But if there be no interpreter," so that man supposed to keep silence in the church, and/or speak to himself and to God because he knows what he is saying, and God knows what he is saying. Verse 29

"Let the prophets speak two or three, and let the other judge." It divides where it says, "let the other judge."

1 Corinthians 12:10

"To another, the working of miracles; to another, prophecy; to another, discerning of spirits; to another, divers kinds of tongues; to another, the interpretation of tongues:" Now the prophets suppose to speak by two or three, but nowadays the prophets want to speak by one. This is why they are false, and there are many false prophets because they want to speak by one. They are not following God's instruction. Now in the New Testament, God sends the prophets by two or three. Now in Revelation chapter 11, God sent the prophets by two, the two witnesses. In Acts, the apostles went out by two or three, Paul and Barnabas. Paul and Silas are found in Acts 15:22-40. You remember when Jesus sent out his disciples, he sent them out by two. That is found in Mark 6:7, Matthew 10:1, and in Luke 10:1. You see how the Lord sends them out by two in the New Testament? The Lord said, "My people are destroyed for lack of knowledge: because thou hast rejected knowledge." Now the prophets suppose to speak by two or three. Now back to speaking in tongue. I heard some of these teachers and preachers say that tongue has been done away with and all the other gifts too, but that is not true. He gave the gift of healing. Not all men can heal, just some. Now teaching is a gift if you teach correctly. If you do not teach correctly, you do not have that gift from God. The Bible says that tongues shall cease. That means that any time in the future, from the time that Paul said it, he did not say all of the rest of the gifts shall cease. These teachers and prophets are all confused, knowledge has vanished from them.

Now I would like to explain more about Daniel 9:27 because people are confused by so many false teachings on this. I made an error on a quote from the Bible on my first book called "The Beast That Was, And Is Not. And Yet Is".

Now many people would like to know about Daniel seventy weeks, especially the last seven years. I will write about this so that you will understand.

Daniel 9:27

"And he shall confirm the convenant with many for one week: and in the midst of the week he shall cause the sacrifice and the oblation to cease, and for the overspreading of abominations, he shall make it desolate, even until the consummation, and that determined shall be poured upon the desolate." Now most of these men, these false prophets, preachers, and teachers say where it says, "and he shall confirm the covenant with many for one week:" they say that is the antichrist in Daniel 9:27, but that is not true. That is when Jesus will confirm the convenant with many for one week. Now you see how these men deceive the people with their lies. Yes, Jesus Christ will confirm the covenant with many for one week. He will send the two witnesses, so he is confirming the covenant; "and in the midst of the week he will cause the sacrifice and oblation to cease" means in the midst of the week the two witnesses will be killed when they finish their testimony. They will prophecy for three and a half years, and after that, the antichrist and his armies will kill the two witnesses. He will then set up an abomination that maketh desolate. It will be that image like Nebuchadnezzar did, and that will last three and a half years. So that makes the one week the last seven years. The two witnesses will prophecy for three and a half years and then be killed. Then after that, the antichrist will rule for three and a half years. That will make the one week, seven years, that Jesus Christ will confirm the covenant with many for one week.

So God will confirm the covenant with his people for one week, the last seven years when the two witnesses come. God's power will be with the two witnesses, his presence, just like when he was with Moses and Aaron; and in the midst of the week the two witnesses will be killed. This is God's doing because in the New Testament the saints are the daily sacrifice. He

123

shall cause the sacrifice and the oblation to cease. That is when the two witnesses will finish their testimony and will be killed. So God allows the beast that ascendeth out of the pit to kill the two witnesses because they have finished their testimony. So God cause the sacrifice and the oblation to cease. Some of the false prophets say that the antichrist cause the sacrifice and the oblation to cease, but that is not true. God cause the sacrifice and the oblation to cease. It's just like God caused Israel, Jerusalem to go into captivity in the first Babylon. He used Nebuchadnezzar to carry them away, captive, from Jerusalem to Babylon. Now turn to Jeremiah 29:1 and I will show you what I am talking about.

Jeremiah 29:1

"Now these are the words of the letter that Jeremiah the prophet sent from Jerusalem unto the residue of the elders which were carried away captives, and to the priests, and to the prophets, and to all the people whom Nebuchadnezzar had carried away captive from Jerusalem to Babylon:" Now you see in this verse, Nebuchadnezzar had carried them away, captive, from Jerusalem to Babylon.

Jeremiah 29:4

"Thus said the LORD of hosts, the God of Israel, unto all that are carried away captives, whom I have caused to be carried away from Jerusalem unto Babylon." So that is the same thing in verse 1 and verse 4. In verse 1 God give Nebuchadnezzar the power to carry them away, captive, from Jerusalem to Babylon. In verse 4 the Bible says God caused them to be carried away from Jerusalem to Babylon. It is just like what you read about in Daniel 9:27 and Daniel 11:31, which is God caused the sacrifice and the ablation to cease. God gives the antichrist power to take away the daily sacrifice, which means to kill the saints and put some in prison.

The antichrist will be making war with the saints. When you make war, what exactly do you do? You kill some, you capture some, and you put some in prison. The Bible says, "And it was given unto him to make war with the saints, and to overcome them:" So it was given unto him by whom? It was given unto him by God. God is causing the sacrifice to cease. Now let's read what God said in Revelation 6:10, 11.

Revelation 6:10

"And they cried with a loud voice, saying, How long, O LORD, holy and true, dost thou not judge and avenge our blood on them that dwell on the earth?"

Revelation 6:11

"And white robes were given unto every one of them; and it was said unto them, that they should rest yet for a little season, until their fellow servants also and their brethren, that they should be killed as they were, should be fulfilled." You see God want a certain amount of saints to be killed, and then it will be fulfilled. So God caused the sacrifice to cease because the daily sacrifice are the saints of God. I hope that everyone understands that.

Remember like Saul did, and his name was changed to Paul. So remember in the new testament Paul was taking away the daily sacrifice. He was hauling off the saints to jail and prison, and some of them were being put to death. This is what the antichrist will do. After they kill the two witnesses, then the antichrist will tell the people that they should make an image to the beast. So the antichrist, the false prophets, will set up an image that everybody should worship, and whosoever would not worship the image of the beast should be killed. That is when the great tribulation starts. There is so much I can tell you and explain Revelation and Daniel.

But I know that some things people will disagree with me because they go about what they have been taught and not by what the bible says. Most people would rather believe their pastor, preachers, or prophets rather than believe the word of God. Many people have no knowledge, no wisdom, or no understanding of the word of God.

Now let's go back to Daniel 9:27 where it says, "the covenant with". It goes to Isaiah 42:6, Isaiah 55:3, Jeremiah 31:31, and Ezekiel 16:60, 61,62.

Now Isaiah 42:6

"I the LORD have called thee in righteousness, and will hold thine hand, and will keep thee, and give thee for a covenant of the people, for a light of the Gintiles;" You see God made a covenant with his people.

Now Isaiah 55:3

"Incline your ear, and come unto me: hear, and your soul shall live; and I will make an everlasting covenant with you, even the sure mercies of David." Now you see that God said that he will make an everlasting covenant with you.

New Jeremiah 31:31

"Behold, the days come, saith the LORD, that I will make a new covenant with the house of Israel, and with the house of Judah:" Now God made a covenant with his people. He will confirm the covenant with the two witnesses when they come, and his presence will be with the two witnesses.

Now Ezekiel 16:60, 61,62

Now verse 60

"Nevertheless, I will remember my covenant with thee in the days of thy youth, and I will establish unto thee an everlasting covenant." Like I said before, the LORD will confirm the covenant with many for one week in Daniel 9:27.

Now verse 61

"Then thou shall remember thy ways, and be ashamed, when thou shalt receive thy sisters, thine elder and thy younger: and I will give them unto thee for daughters, but not by thy covenant." You see the LORD will establish his covenant with his people.

Now verse 62

"And I will establish my covenant with thee; and thou shalt know that I am the LORD:" You see in Daniel 9:27 this is the LORD, Jesus, confirming the covenant with many for one week.

The next dividing of the word of truth in Daniel 9:27 where it says, "many for one week:" One week is seven years, and that's the last seven years, then Jesus will come.

Remember what Jesus said in Matthew chapter 24:15. He said, "When ye, therefore, shall see the abomination of desolation, spoken of by Daniel the prophet, stand in the holy place, (whoso readeth, let him understand)". Now, Jesus is talking about the end time in Matthew 24. So he will confirm the covenant with many for one week, and the abomination that maketh desolate all will be in that seven years period of time. At the end of the first three and a half years, the two witnesses will be killed, and the last three and a half years, the antichrist will set up an abomination that maketh desolate.

Now Daniel 9:27 where it says, "many for one week", for more insight turn to Isaiah 53:11, Matthew 26:28, Romans 5:15 and 19, Hebrew 9:28.

Now Isaiah 53:11

"He shall see of the travail of his soul, and shall be satisfied: by his knowledge shall my righteous servant justify many; for he shall bear their iniquities." The LORD made a covenant with many.

Now Matthew 26:28

"For this is my blood of the new testament, which is shed for many for the remission of sins." It is Jesus Christ that made the covenant with many for one week. Now some of these false prophets, preachers, teachers say that's the antichrist that made the covenant with many for one week, but that is not true. These men are deceivers. It is Jesus Christ that will confirm the covenant with many for one week.

Now Romans 5:15, 19

Verse 15

"But not as the offense, so also is the free gift, for if through the offence of one many be dead, much more the grace of God, and the gift by grace, which is by one man, Jesus Christ, hath abounded unto many." It is Jesus will confirm the covenant with many for one week.

Now verse 19.

"For as by one man's disobedience many were made sinners, so by the obedience of one shall many be made righteous." By Jesus Christ's obedience, many were made righteous that he confirmed the covenant with.

Now Hebrews 9:28

"So Christ was once offered to bear the sins of many; and unto them that look for him shall he appear the second time without sin unto salvation." Now Christ was once offered to bear the sins of many, the elect, the one hundred forty four thousand.

Now back to Daniel 9:27, where it says, "he shall cause the sacrifice and the ablation to cease, and for the overspreading of the abominations, he shall make it desolate," Now most of these men say that it is the antichrist. These false preachers, teachers, and prophets say that in the antichrist. He shall cause the sacrifice and the oblation to cease, and for the overspreading of abominations, he shall make it desolate, but that is not true. God cause the sacrifice and the oblation to cease, and for the overspreading of abominations, he shall make it desolate. God will make the land desolate for the overspreading of abominations everywhere idols, images, homosexuality, women dressing like men, and men dressing like women. These are all abominations to God. So God will make the land desolate. For more insight let's turn to Ezekiel 33:28,29

Ezekiel 33:28

"For I will lay the land most desolate and the pomp of her strength shall cease; and the mountains of Israel shall be desolate, that none shall pass through."

Ezekiel 33:29

"Then shall they know that I am the LORD, When I have laid the land most desolate because of all their abominations, which they have committed." You see here that God made the land desolate because of all their abominations, which they have committed. Some of these men, false prophets, preachers, and teachers say that this is the antichrist, but that is not true. They don't know the scripture so they are deceived. They continue to deceive others with their lies. You can see for yourself who is telling the truth.

Now back to Daniel 9:27. Let's rightly divide the word of truth where it says, "abomination, he shall make it desolate,". For further insight, let's turn toMatthew 24:15, Mark 13:14, Luke 21:20.

Now Matthew 24:15

"When ye, therefore, shall see the abomination of desolation, spoken of by Daniel the prophet, stand in the holy place, (whoso readeth, let him understand,)" Some of these false prophets say that's when the Jews go back to sacrificing animal sacrifices; and that will make the abomination that maketh desolate, but that is not true. This false prophet from South Carolina says that the Jews will go back to animal sacrifices. They will try to find them a red heifer and go back to the daily sacrifice. Again that is not true because the red heifer was not a daily sacrifice. It was for a water of separation. It is a purification for sin. He that toucheth the dead body of any man shall be unclean seven days. You see, the ashes of the red heifer is a purification for sin. For a better understanding, let's read Numbers 19:12.

Now Numbers 19:12

"He shall purify himself with it on the third day, and on the seventh day he shall be clean: but if he purify not himself the third day, then the seventh day he shall not be clean." Now you see how these false prophets lie to the people. The red heifer was not a daily sacrifice. There are so many false prophets, preachers, and teachers, and they deceive many. The bible talks about the red heifer in Numbers 19. Now let's go back to Mark 13:14.

Now Mark 13:14

"But when ye shall see the abomination of desolation, spoken of by Daniel the prophet, standing where it ought not, (let him that readeth understand,) then let them that be in Judea flee to the mountains:" That is when they set up the image. It is the antichrist, the false prophet, or also known as the second beast in Revelation 13:11. He tells people that they should make an image to the beast, the first beast, that was wounded by a sword and lived. They will then make an image to that beast and that will make the abomination that maketh desolate.

Now Luke 21:20

"And when ye shall see Jerusalem encompassed with armies, then know that the desolation thereof is nigh." That is when the antichrist will have his armies around Jerusalem, and they will take away the daily sacrifice. This means that they will take away the saints. They will kill the two witnesses, and some of the saints, and some will be put in prison. When they kill the two witnesses, then the antichrist will set up the abomination that maketh desolate. That is what we read about in Daniel 11:31. And arms shall stand on his part. The arms mean armies, the ten kings. They shall pollute the sanctuary of strength, and shall take away the daily sacrifice. That means that they will kill the witnesses. They shall place the abomination that maketh desolate. That means they will set up an image like Nebuchadnezzar did and that will start the great tribulation. He wants all nations, languages, people, and tongues to worship that image.

One man, R.G. Stair, that came on his talk show program says that Jerusalem will go into captivity in two thousand thirteen, but that is absolutely not true. That information is false because we are still in the first beast, the lion with eagle wings. Jerusalem will go into captivity after they kill the two witnesses or during the time they kill the two witnesses. That will happen during the fourth beast, and that will happen after the ten kings show up. Then the little horn will get with the ten kings. The little horn is the false prophet.

The false prophet from South Carolina also said that Jesus was going to come by the year two thousand or before, and now he says by the year two thousand thirteen on another tape. He said the world won't make it to two thousand sixteen, but I have all what he said on tape. Now when these years come to pass he will bump it farther back and say that he never said that. I have never heard a false prophet that can lie so much like R.G. Stair, from South Carolina.

Now Daniel 9:27 where it says, "even until the consummation, and that determined shall be poured upon the desolate" For more insight let's read Isaiah 10:22,23, Isaiah 28:22. Daniel 11:36, Luke 21:24, and Romans 11:26.

Now Isaiah 10:22, 23

Verse 22

"For though thy people Israel be as the sand of the sea, yet a remnant of them shall return: the consumption decreed shall overflow with righteousness."

Verse 23

"For the Lord God of hosts shall make a consumption, even determined, in the midst of all the land." Only the remnant, the Lord, will save the one hundred forty four thousand.

Now let's read Lake 21:24

"And they shall fall by the edge of the sword, and shall be led away captive into all nations: and Jerusalem shall be trodden down of the Gentiles, until the times of the Gentiles be fulfilled." Now you see that Jerusalem shall be trodden down of the Gentiles for three and a half years, and that is when the great tribulation will start. Those that are in Judea will have to flee into the mountains for three and a half years. God has a place prepared for them for three and a half years.

Now Ezekiel 38:11, 12 some of these preachers, teachers, and prophets say that it is the United States. They say that because the United States has unwalled villages, but that is not what the bible is talking about. The bible is talking about the land of Israel and his people in verse 11 and 12. This is when the great tribulation will start. When they set up that image, then that the start of the great tribulation, and those that are in Judea have to flee into the mountains. These are the unwalled villages where God has a place prepared for them for three and a half years. At the end of the three and a half years, Gog, the chief prince of Meshech and tubal will come against God's people that fled into the mountains and the unwalled villages. I will explain more to you at another time if it be the will of the LORD. May God bless you all.